DESERT LIVING

Contemplative Living as the Context for Contemplative Praying

Fr. Steven Scherrer, ThD

Preface by
Paul A. and Karen Karper Fredette
Authors of *Consider the Ravens: On Contemporary Hermit Life*

iUniverse, Inc.
New York   Bloomington

Desert Living
Contemplative Living as the Context for Contemplative Praying

iUniverse books may be ordered through booksellers or by contacting:

iUniverse
1663 Liberty Drive
Bloomington, IN 47403
www.iuniverse.com
1-800-Authors (1-800-288-4677)

ISBN: 978-1-4401-7655-5 (pbk)
ISBN: 978-1-4401-7657-9 (cloth)
ISBN: 978-1-4401-7656-2 (ebook)

Library of Congress Control Number: 2009937132

Printed in the United States of America

iUniverse rev. date: 10/15/09

Contents

Part III: The Desert Aroma: The Mystical Dimension of Desert Living

Preface

"There are many who live in the mountains and behave as if they were in the town, and they are wasting their time. It is possible to be a solitary in one's mind while living in a crowd, and it is possible for one who is a solitary to live in the crowd of his own thoughts." (Amma Syncletica, *The Sayings of the Desert Fathers, The Alphabetical Collection,* Trans. Benedicta Ward, SLG, p.234)

A more modern "Saying" reads thus: It is not the place that makes the hermit but rather the hermit who makes the place (a hermitage). Fr. Steven Scherrer is addressing any of us who experience an attraction to solitude and silence but are committed by either love or necessity to a life in the often hectic and noisy secular world. In his thoughtful and original chapters, Fr. Scherrer challenges us to discern whether our attraction is based in reality or is simply a romantic notion that we like to trot out for discussion with a spiritual guide. It is lovely to envision one's self in a cabin tucked away in the wilderness where we live without disturbance, spending our days and nights caught up in sweet rapture. Pesky questions such as "What shall I eat?" or "What shall I wear?" do not arise to disturb our idyllic rest in the Lord.

The real question should be: "When shall I pray?" The answer is simple: Now! As to "Where?" the answer should be: Here! We do not need to go off into a literal desert in order to become a hermit at heart. Solitary moments can be found in almost everyone's day and if used wisely, can ground us in our inner hermitage where we can entertain the Lord like Martha and also listen to his voice like Mary. If we are to attain the goal of contemplative prayer, we have to *live* contemplatively, i.e. with as little outer or inner noise as possible.

As Fr. Scherrer exemplifies in his own life, we can begin by leaving the TV screen dark; flicking off the car radio; cutting back on unnecessary socializing and turning off our cell phone, that devious device through which people can invade what little solitude we may have garnered. Before long, we will seek out solitude with the focus of one panning for gold amidst the silt of our daily grind. When it doesn't turn up on its own, we will employ more positive measures to recover "the treasure hidden in the field" of our lives.

We will begin savoring our daily commute which affords us quiet time to muse over our distresses and delights in the company of the One who provides the ultimate in listening pleasure/experience. If we are naturally a morning person, we may elect to wake up a half-hour before the rest of our household begins to stir and prepare ourselves for the day by discussing our concerns for family and friends with the most compassionate of all Friends. For those of us who are night owls, the hour after our household has retired can become a valuable opportunity for a contemplative review of where we are and where we are going.

What would our life be like if we reduced the time currently employed tapping on our laptop, instant messaging with our blackberry or tweeting with other twitterers, and spent more time in silence, solitude, stillness? Occasionally it takes the shock of realizing we are running on empty before we heed the invitation to "Come away to a desert place," as Fr. Scherrer encourages us to do and prepare for contemplative prayer through contemplative living.

August 22, 2009
Feast of the Queenship of Mary
Paul A. & Karen Karper Fredette

Introduction

Desert Living is a collection of my essays and sermons on the theme of religious life—understood in the broad sense—including the diocesan priesthood, societies of apostolic life, as well as formal religious orders. It is particularly geared toward the eremitic or solitary life, a life of prayer and fasting in the desert, far from the world.

Each chapter is a complete unit. This necessarily involves a certain amount of repetition, since the individual chapters were originally written for ever new audiences. Yet, I believe that a compilation of this sort has certain advantages. For one thing, it keeps the basic elements ever before our eyes, for I continue to look at the same, basic, fundamental points from ever new perspectives, instead of simply making a key point and then moving on to other matters. *Desert Living* is an extended meditation on the mystery of religious, monastic, and eremitic life. A good preacher repeats his basic and most fundamental points often because he knows his audience and their needs. Since it is my concern to communicate a basic, life-giving message, I feel that this approach is particularly suitable for this purpose.

As the first chapter explains, I have long been concerned with the issues involved in *Desert Living*. Many today are interested in contemplative *prayer*, but few in contemplative *living*, which is the context within which contemplative prayer can grow, flourish, and fill our life. The connection between contemplative praying and contemplative living is the main issue I am concerned with in *Desert Living*. Contemplative living is desert living, ascetical living, a simple, plain, unadorned life, devoted wholeheartedly to the love of God beyond all other things.

In part one, I deal with the basic principles involved in the ascetical-mystical life. The longest chapter is on the fundamental principles of Christian spirituality seen through the writings of St. John of the Cross. I also discuss other issues, such as the dying of religious orders and societies of apostolic life in our day. I look at the causes of the present-day drastic fall off in vocations to the priesthood and religious life. I deal with issues such as the meaning of celibacy, evangelical poverty, religious dress, fasting, asceticism, and contemplative prayer in religious life today. Of particular interest to me is the life of those who are retired. I consider this from the point of view of a life of *religious* retirement and contrast it with the secular model of retirement.

In part two, I am especially concerned with the Biblical roots of the *ascetical* dimension of the ascetical-mystical life and how we live out this dimension.

I believe that the Church today needs to be renewed through fresh Biblical reflection on the basic principles involved in religious life. We then need to put into practice these basic, Biblical principles. In *Desert Living* I seek to do this Biblical reflection and to point out practical ways to live it.

In part three I focus on the *mystical* dimension of the ascetical-mystical life and look particularly at St. Joseph, the Virgin Mary, and St. Bernard of Clairvaux as examples of mystical contemplation. The imagery of the Canticle of Canticles is particularly helpful here.

Finally, I include an appendix of key texts of official Church teaching on celibacy as compared with marriage in order to put my general approach within the context of Church teaching on the excellence of religious life as a privileged way of growing in Christian holiness.

Fr. Steven Scherrer, MM
Memorial of Saint Bernard of Clairvaux
August 20, 2009
Ossining, New York

Part I
The Desert Life: The Basic Principles of Desert Living

DESERT LIVING

Born in 1945, I have long felt called to a monastic and even hermit life, and I have lived nearly fourteen years in various contemplative and eremitic (desert/hermit) monasteries. I was ordained a Catholic priest in 1972, and of my thirty-seven years of priesthood, I have spent the last twenty-seven of them on this quest. I received a doctorate in New Testament (ThD) from Harvard University in 1979, and did missionary work among the nomadic Turkana people of Kenya's Northern Frontier District (Lodwar) for seven years. I fell in love with the desert at that time. I am now living a contemplative, monastic life in Ossining, New York. In *Desert Life,* I work out my understanding of the desert/hermit life.

My desert quest began twenty-seven years ago, in 1982, when I was thirty-seven years old, while teaching New Testament at the major seminary in Dar es Salaam, Tanzania, when I read a biography of Charles de Foucauld, a French priest/hermit in the Sahara (died 1916). His contemplative, desert life utterly fascinated me. He lived among the nomadic Tuareg people, leading a life of prayer, fasting, renunciation of the world, and missionary zeal to spread the love of Christ among that people.

I decided then and there that this would henceforth be my life. God was transforming me at that time, and I began to make many radical changes in my life. I gave up meat and greatly simplified my diet and life in general, eliminating recreational trips and all things worldly in order to have an undivided heart in my love for God.

As you might well imagine, even the first steps of such a new way of life, as I was then, under God's guidance, beginning to develop it, were met with astonishment and dismay. Yet these beginnings led me to visit the Egyptian desert monasteries of Baramus and Macarius in Scetis, in the Wadi Natrun, and to work and live myself for seven years among the nomadic Turkana tribe in the desert of northern Kenya (Lodwar). Finally, I was led to an eremitic monastery in the United States, where I spent five years, and then to three cenobitic monasteries, where I spent another nine years. One of these latter was a female monastery in Venezuela, over which I was appointed chaplain for four years. A disease in my feet, legs, and hands (peripheral neuropathy), which began about five years ago, finally forced me to return to my original religious community about a year ago and retire at age sixty-three. Now, at last, I am finally fully free to live according to my desert/hermit ideals.

I can truly say that living in this place as a retired priest seems to be an ideal setting for me to live a hermit life, as I believe God is inspiring me to live it, particularly in terms of separation from the world.

Separation from the world is an essential characteristic of the hermit because it enables him to live for God alone with an undivided heart, i.e. to keep his heart from being distracted, dissipated, and divided by the many distractions, attractions, pleasures, and loves of this world.

How do I live in separation from the world? Well, I have no telephone, and I have reserved my room as a private hermitage for prayer, reading, study, and writing. I do not receive visitors in my room. I also keep strict silence—not leaving my room—every day from seven thirty in the evening until noon of the following day. I keep strict silence as well in certain areas of this building, namely on the stairways and above the first floor in general, i.e. where the men have their rooms, except in obvious talking areas, such as the parlors. I take my one daily meal with the other priests and brothers who live in this house, and enjoy conversing with them at that meal.

I avoid worldly pleasures in general in order to devote myself to God with an undivided heart. For me, that means no television or movies, no radio, no reading of newspapers, no drinking or smoking, or going out to eat in restaurants. I eat only simple, healthy foods, without meat or any seasoning, except salt. I eat nothing fried, nothing made of white flour, and no white rice. I consider white flour and white rice inappropriate foods for contemplatives, for the most nutritious part has been removed to increase pleasure. Contemplatives are those who renounce the pleasures of this world in order to find their pleasure only in God, to the degree that that is possible. I also eat nothing containing added sugar or artificial sweeteners, and no delicacies (no ice cream, cakes, pies, cookies, etc., not even sugar-free) in order to seek pleasure only in God.

I eat only once a day, at midday, in order not to be weighed down by undigested food from three in the morning until noon, which is my most important time for prayer, contemplation, *lectio divina*, and spiritual work. I found that breakfast drops me spiritually at my most intense spiritual time. I also found that supper very often leaves me heavy and weighed down, still digesting food at three in the morning when I rise for prayer.

I have no car and I no longer drive. I take no trips outside of this house, except to the doctor, but I do walk around its beautiful grounds. I say a private Mass daily at seven in the morning, in a small chapel, and slowly pray the full liturgy of the hours, including the three little hours.

My ideal is basically to live alone with God in silence, prayer, reading, and writing. I share my daily sermons and other writings in English and Spanish through group e-mails and on a website (www.DailyBiblicalSermons.com). I also give printed copies of my daily sermons to those in this house that are interested but do not have computers. I feel that writing is now my main work and ministry, along with trying to spread the love of Christ to all with whom I have personal contact, mainly at the noon meal. I hope by my prayer, example of life, love, and writings that I may help others.

I also always wear clerical dress. Clerical or religious dress has been my only way of dressing for the past twenty years (I was ordained thirty-seven years ago). This way of dressing distinguishes who I am, gives public witness to my ideals, and also further separates me from the world. This witness, I believe, reminds the world of God and spiritual things, to its benefit.

Is Religious Life Dying in the United States Today?

When we look around us year after year and see our religious societies, communities, and orders shrinking more and more, with practically no new recruits, we are bound to ask ourselves what is going on and why. I myself find this to be a frequent topic of conversation at table, but I almost never hear anything that strikes me as the answer or reason for what is happening. We are like the *Titanic* going down, and no one seems to know why, or what can be done to reverse the situation, or if it is even possible to reverse it.

My own approach, though, is to look at what we once were when our numbers were large and vocations booming, and compare that with what we now are. If we do that, I think we can discover the direction in which we need to move. It is not just a simple matter of returning to what we once were, to be sure, but I do believe that there is something we can learn by making that comparison. I think we can discover thereby the type of changes we should now be making.

The priesthood in general, as well as religious life, once had a rather sharply defined and very visible religious or monastic dimension—for want of a better term—a certain something that was once very important but which is now disappearing. It included very visible things, such as clerical or religious dress or habit, which very much defined how we lived, what we did, and what we did not feel comfortable doing.

I use the term *religious life* here in the broad sense to include the sisters who once taught in our schools as well as societies of apostolic life and the diocesan priesthood, even though these are not all religious orders in the technical sense.

I think what I am trying to say is that we once had a way of life to a far greater extent than we do now. We could even speak with a certain pride about the clerical way of life, a term which is now quite pejorative, something that many today simply reject altogether. But I think that this is precisely where our problem lies. We have, I believe, lost the sense that the priesthood

6

is indeed a whole way of life that sets norms for our behavior, our way of living, our way of dressing, things we do, and things we have given up doing for the love of God and for the love of this new way of life that God has called us to and that we have taken up.

We find ourselves today stressing freedom and using it to be just like the world around us, imitating its way of life, from the clothes one wears to the food one eats and the TV shows and movies one watches—none of which could be called a religious way of life or a distinctively different way of life at all. And so young people visit our modern communities, and in one minute they see the most visible things—namely, how they dress and what they eat—and can deduce rather quickly that this community does not appear to be a religious community, as they were expecting it to be. When looking at our modern communities, they too often fail to see evidence of a special way of life, of a priestly or religious way of life as a whole way of living and as a witness to the world of very different values and beliefs from what one finds in the world around us. And so most of these young people do not come back, and we do not grow. Is this not the situation that we are now in, in the Church today? And does this not remarkably contrast with what we once were? And what is the point of the contrast? Is it not the religious element, the whole-way-of-life element that seems to be lacking? Is it not what I think we might even call the monastic element, which we once had, that is missing today?

Christ calls all to perfection. Everyone should feel himself or herself addressed and challenged by the call of the rich young man (Mt 19:21), not just priests and religious and members of societies of apostolic life. Yet we who belong to these societies or orders should also feel ourselves very much addressed and challenged by this call to perfection given to the rich young man. We should feel this call in our own unique way as celibates following Christ in simplicity and evangelical poverty, renouncing the pleasures of this world for those of the Kingdom of God and giving up the delights of *this* creation for those of the *new* creation. We, as religious—even though not necessarily religious in the technical sense—seek to follow Christ in a specific way, with a radically undivided heart, not even divided by Christian marriage and family. As religious, we seek to love God with our whole heart in a truly radical way that is expressed in our whole way of life. We express this radical love in the way we dress as priests and religious, in the simplicity of our meals, and in the silence and sobriety for prayer in which we live. We also express our radical, wholehearted love of God in our renunciation of worldly pleasures and of the ways of the world in general.

People should be able to come into one of our houses and at once sense the difference between our life and that of the world around us. The externals of our way of life—which are the first things that one notices—should be true expressions of our inner priestly and religious spirit and way of living. People could once sense this almost immediately upon entering one of our houses. Do they sense it today? I think that if you, in all honesty, have to answer no, you have just put your finger on where we now need to begin to look for the hole in the bow of the *Titanic*, before we go down altogether. It is this monastic, religious, or priestly aspect of our life as a whole way of life that we need to work on from the inside out, from its inner principles to its outer expressions, signs, and practices. This is, I believe, the direction in which we now need to move in priestly and religious life in the United States today.

Religious Dress

Are we not beginning to see signs here and there today of a possible comeback of religious dress in religious life? I use the term *religious life* here in an open sense which includes all forms of celibate life for the Kingdom. By *religious dress* I mean a black suit with a Roman collar or a cassock for priests, and a religious habit or clerical suit for members of formal religious orders.

There was once a time, which many of us still remember, forty years and more ago, when all of us who were members of religious institutes or societies of apostolic life wore a distinctive cassock or habit practically all the time when we were in our religious or society houses in this country. But then came the year 1967 in which, in our institute, our distinctive cassock was abandoned by practically everyone in order to update our society in accord with the desires of Vatican II, which had just ended.

The clergyman, tab-collared, clerical shirt, if you remember, was invented and introduced around the year 1966, and at first, for a few years it was worn with a black suit as a replacement for the cassock. But in several years time that too began to disappear as a regular form of clerical dress in our houses, until almost no one wore clerical dress any more on a regular basis in our houses. Religious dress was for all practical purposes reserved for funerals and Sunday Mass help outs.

If someone wears a back suit with a Roman collar today in one of our houses, he really stands out. At first, people will think that he has probably just come back from a funeral or an outside Mass. But if he continues to wear it for several days in a row, he will surely be the only one in the house who does so, and will be very conspicuous indeed. The norm nowadays is secular dress, and in the summer, some even wear shorts. Where we once had a strict dress code in our houses, we certainly have none now.

So that is where we are at today, but is this really the ideal? According to the new code of Canon Law, published in 1983, when all dress codes had already become ancient history in our institute at least, the ideal is stated rather differently. Canon 284 reads: "Clerics are to wear suitable ecclesiastical dress, in accordance with the norms established by the Episcopal Conference and legitimate local custom." If "legitimate local custom" intends to mean secular dress, then this canon is meaningless, and need not have been written or included in the new code. "Suitable ecclesiastical dress" in the United States has always been a cassock, a black suit worn with a Roman collar, or a religious habit (Coriden, 220). What "suitable ecclesiastical dress" means today can be surmised from the norms issued for both diocesan and religious priests of the diocese of Rome, namely, the cassock or dark-colored clerical suit with an ecclesiastical Roman collar. Religious are to wear their habit or the clerical suit. These norms, issued by the vicar of Rome, Cardinal Poletti, on October 1, 1982, were approved by the Holy Father on September 27, 1982 (Coriden, 221).

Religious dress is, in fact, I believe, a help to us in living a religious life—again understood as including all who have dedicated themselves to a life of celibacy for the Kingdom within some ecclesiastical institute. Religious dress, whether it be a black suit and Roman collar, a cassock, or a religious habit, gives us identity, constantly reminding ourselves and others of who we are and of how we have publicly dedicated our lives. It separates us from the world in a good sense—that is, from false and worldly values. It even makes us look and feel out of place, uncomfortable, and conspicuous in certain places—even innocent places—where it would be better were we not present.

Religious dress helps us to live a more dedicated life, namely, a life fully devoted to Christ, a life of prayer, recollection, spiritual reading, sacrifice, self-denial, and ministry. It also gives witness to others, reminding them of God, and of the ideals that the priesthood and religious life stand for. We are to give witness in the world to Christ by our words and by the example of our life; and religious dress helps us to do so.

Religious dress is, furthermore, a symbol; and symbols are important. We need symbols. We live by symbols. We do not just invent symbols. True and meaningful symbols, especially religious symbols, are rooted in history, in the past, and they speak by themselves, without need of explanation. Religion in particular needs symbols. Symbols speak directly to the heart, rather than only to the mind. Religious dress is such a symbol. It stands for a whole set of publicly, culturally, and religiously known ideals and values. It symbolizes a whole way of life, a way of being in the world, a new way of living in the world. Religious dress reminds us—if we dress this way—and others who see us of these values.

Religious dress speaks of a life of dedication, a life with an undivided heart, reserved only for the Lord; and it speaks of a way of living that is congruent with these values. We ourselves constantly need to be reminded of these values, and should be living them. Religious dress helps us in this, reminding both ourselves and others that we are trying to live sacrificially for the Lord and his ministry, renouncing the pleasures of this world and of this creation for the greater and purer joys of the Kingdom of God and of the new creation. It reminds us and others that we are to love God with all our heart and soul, all our mind and strength (Mk 12:30).

Having said all this, I wonder whether we might not begin to see something new in our own time, something that we rarely saw even before 1967, that is, those who wear religious dress all the time. Would this not be an even greater symbol? Sisters once lived that way. You never saw them in secular dress before 1967. Hence the symbolism of their habit had great impact. This was more unusual for priests and male religious even before 1967, but is this not the ideal and the direction in which we ought be looking and moving today? Hence, I am not just talking about a simple restoration of past practice, but rather of a meaningful ideal from the past which we ought to reexamine, understand more deeply, and begin to live in a new and fresh way, a way that is more meaningful and radical than the way most lived it even before 1967.

Contemplative Living as the Context for Contemplative Praying

There is much new interest in contemplative prayer today within religious communities and societies of apostolic life.

Prayer is communication and relationship with God and it has a variety of forms: the divine office, the eucharist, meditation on scripture, memorized prayers, prayers in our own words, and contemplative prayer.

I would like to focus here on contemplative prayer.

Contemplative prayer is a wordless, imageless communication with God in love, light, and heavenly peace, when God so deigns to grant us this gift. Yet we can also do our part to prepare the way for contemplative prayer by sitting quietly and waiting in silence every day, perhaps focusing ourselves by using the Jesus prayer. Although the Jesus prayer uses words as an initial preparation for contemplative prayer, it is nonetheless a constant repetition of the same words, and so it helps us to keep out more serious distractions while at the same time focusing us on God. It is something like white noise, which blocks out more disturbing exterior sounds.

All forms of prayer are necessary and important, and they help each other. But the goal is that they should all lead us to an ever richer living experience of the love of God in the heart. The practice of sitting quietly and waiting for or experiencing contemplative prayer should deepen all our forms of prayer.

The key to contemplative prayer is to empty ourselves so that God can fill us with himself. If you are full of distracting images from watching television, for example, you will probably not make much progress in contemplation or as a contemplative. That is why the context of our way of living is so important for contemplatives. For this reason, monks, devoted to the contemplative life, separate themselves from the world, with all its entertainments and distractions. That is why they live in silence; eat simple, basic, meatless meals; and live within a monastic enclosure. They realize that a life dedicated to contemplation involves the *whole* of one's self, the *whole* of one's life. It is a whole way of life. It is far more than just learning some sitting and breathing techniques to be used for some hours each day when we devote ourselves to contemplative prayer. A whole contemplative way of living is the necessary context for fruitful contemplative praying.

In contemplative praying, we do our part; and when God sees that we are ready, he does his part. Our part consists in our whole way of life, as well as in sitting in a dimly lit room in silence with our eyes closed and our head bowed, repeating the Jesus prayer or something similar. God then does the rest. Most often, he will just let us sit peacefully and prayerfully with him; but at other times, he will suddenly reveal himself, filling our whole being with light, love, and heavenly peace and joy. This may last for about a half hour or an hour, but it gradually overflows into our whole day and life, allowing us to walk in the happiness of the splendor of Christ. Some may only rarely experience this prayer of union. Others experience it frequently. That is God's decision; but our preparation for it is also important. Those who prepare for it by their contemplative way of living and wait daily to receive it are more likely to experience it more often.

Concerning contemplative living, those who are serious about contemplative praying will pay much attention to it, for they know what an essential part it plays. Many will, therefore, rise early to start their day with silent prayer, the divine office, the eucharist, and *lectio divina*. They will also pay careful attention to the way they eat, knowing that unnecessary pleasures outside of God only diminish the pleasure they will find in God. St. Bernard's monks, therefore, banned from their refectory all delicacies, including white bread, even on solemnities, considering it to be a delicacy inappropriate for monks and contemplatives, since the most nutritious part has been removed only to increase the pleasure of eating. There is no need then to say anything further about cakes, pies, cookies, ice cream, whipped cream, etc.—even sugar free. St. Bernard's monks furthermore seasoned their food only with salt (which is necessary for life), and avoided meat and fried foods (see his *First Letter* #11–12; 20). They were serious about not seeking unnecessary pleasures outside of God so that they could find all the more pleasure in God himself, whom they sought to love with their whole heart, without any division.

Television is also something that monks renounce as a source of entertainment inappropriate for contemplatives seeking to empty their minds and hearts of unnecessary stimuli so that their whole life becomes contemplative, full of God.

Such then is a life full of contemplation, full of God. One's whole life is thus lived contemplatively in silence and renunciation of the pleasures of this world.

The splendor of our contemplation then overflows into our whole life, while our whole life forms the nurturing context within which contemplative prayer flourishes.

ST. BRUNO'S LIFE OF
RELIGIOUS RETIREMENT

"You shall love the Lord your God with all your heart, and with all your soul, and with all your strength, and with all your mind; and your neighbor as yourself" (Lk 10:27).

This is the answer to the question, "Teacher, what shall I do to inherit eternal life?" (Lk 10:25). This is the way of life, the straight and narrow way of life, that few find (Mt 7:13–14). This is the way of the undivided heart, for he who loves God with *all* his heart loves him with an undivided heart. All are called to live this way, and those who do so more radically have a higher from of life (see the Appendix on this point).

St. Bruno founded the Carthusian Order in 1084, near Grenoble, France. He was German by birth, born in Cologne, Germany, but was for many years a professor of Sacred Scripture in Rheims, France. At about age fifty, he decided to leave the world to live a solitary life in the wilderness, in order to dedicate himself more strictly and directly to God with all his heart, all his soul, all his strength, and all his mind. He therefore stopped teaching Scripture and began his life anew, in his early fifties, with several companions, in the wilderness of the Grande Chartreuse. He devoted himself to prayer, chanting the divine office, spiritual reading, spiritual study, and some manual labor in great silence, far from the world and its distractions, attractions, and temptations that divide the heart.

Have you ever felt a similar call to serve God alone, more directly and more radically in this way? If you are retired, you now have a unique and marvelous opportunity to do just that: to retire from the world, to live from now on a life of *religious* retirement. You are now finally free from all other obligations. You have a place to live and food to eat, and no longer have to work for a living. If you are a priest, a religious, or are single, you can live such a life in an even more radical way (see the Appendix). You can use this final period of your life to love God with all your heart, all your strength, all your soul, and all your mind in a direct way, as did St. Bruno, once he had retired from teaching Sacred Scripture.

St. Bruno was doing well and was doing much good for God and the Church as a professor of Sacred Scripture, but he did better focusing himself directly on God without other distractions, pleasures, trips, or the delights of the table. He was now living a life of strict and constant fasting, in solitude, in the wilderness, in great silence and recollection. It was a life with God, with an undivided heart, in profound silence and recollection.

If you are retired, you can also retire from the world, if you want to. You now have a new and unique opportunity to do so, leaving behind television, movies, the delights of the table, and other diversions, secular pastimes, recreations, and games, in order to live now, during this final period of your life, with God alone in a unique and radical way.

If you decide to do this, you will also be of the greatest possible service to your neighbor as well through your life of prayer and union with God— which raises the general spiritual level of everyone—through the testimony of your word, through the example of your way of life, and, if you write, through your writings.

A LIFE OF
RELIGIOUS RETIREMENT
This chapter was originally written for retired priests and brothers.

I

TWO ASPECTS OF CONTEMPLATION

Even though many of us have an active spirituality, I believe that many also have a contemplative bent, a deep-down longing for a more contemplative life of prayer, union, and inner peace with God, both during our prayer time and in our whole life.

But then suddenly, having been trained with an active spirituality, we now find ourselves retired, and many of us now have some physical disability as well, which greatly limits our ability to do active ministry. In terms of our active life, active training, and active spirituality, we seem to have fallen by the wayside as the world moves ahead and others pass us by.

Yet from another point of view, I believe that we are not at all at a disadvantage in being retired. And this other point of view is really the most important point of view of all; according it, we are actually in a most important phase of our life at this time of retirement, with our limiting physical disabilities. We are now, in fact, in an ideal situation for contemplative living, which is a life of *religious* retirement.

The problem, though, is that many of us have had little training for this and may know little about the basic principles involved in contemplative living and praying. We were not trained for this in the seminary, and many have not done much reading since about the contemplative life, contemplative spirituality, contemplative living, or contemplative prayer. Yet now we have an ideal opportunity, which few in active ministry have, to live a contemplative life, a life of *religious* retirement. It is a great shame that so few know much about contemplative living and praying and its basic principles, for this is one of the few really worthwhile things that we can still do, and do supremely well, at this point in our life.

The only other viable alternative to living a contemplative life, when we can do little else, is to try to imitate the secular model of retirement, which is basically a life of fun and games, dedicated to entertainment, television, movies, fine dining, and a generally self-centered, pleasure-seeking, materialistic way of living. But is this really what we want for ourselves as priests and brothers at this important time of our life? Is this really what God wants for us now? Is this really suitable for us at this final point of our life, when we should be preparing to meet God? Is this really God's plan for this final time, after a hard-working life as a clergyman or religious?

Is it not rather God's plan that after such an active life of ministry, we should now have some quiet, secluded years, devoted to seeking God in silence, solitude, and simplicity of life? In this way we can experience a deeper union with God in the scriptures, in the Mass, in the divine office, in our reading, in our meditation, and in our daily contemplative prayer. Is this not the direction that our life should now be taking? As retired priests and brothers, we now have a unique opportunity to pursue a quiet life of inner peace and spiritual joy, a life of union with God, from which we can also reflect the love of God to others, and so become ourselves a spiritual blessing for all (Phil 2:15), raising the spiritual level of the world in general.

But what are the basic spiritual principles involved in such a life, principles which we need to learn in order to be able to live well this life of contemplation and *religious* retirement? The goal of such a life, for which we are now ideally suited, is to enter into a deep and wordless communion with God in our heart in silent prayer, in which we experience deep inner peace, joy, and spiritual love. This then overflows into our whole life, giving it a spiritual sweetness and light not of this world.

This is the goal, but to achieve it we must do two things. We must focus on our way of praying and on our way of living.

In terms of our way of praying, we need to sit regularly, daily, in silence, with our eyes closed, focused on the Lord in love and self-gift, emptying our mind of other thoughts, and offering ourselves to God in love. This emptying of the mind is usually done by using the Jesus prayer, or some similar, short, repeated ejaculatory prayer, which helps us block out distracting thoughts while at the same time focusing our mind and heart on God in loving self-offering. At times, such a prayer will lead us into a genuine experience of God's loving, illumining, refreshing presence within us. At other times, there will be no special experience connected with it, but it will nonetheless be a useful and valuable time spent with the Lord, which will help prepare us for entering into a real contemplative experience of him at some future time, when he deigns to grant it to us. This then we can call the first principle of the contemplative life, which we must learn and begin to practice regularly if we want to live and pray contemplatively in a genuine life of religious retirement.

But then there is a second point that we also need to learn and begin to practice if we want to become contemplatives, living a life of religious retirement. And this second point is that we need to focus on our way of living. This includes our whole day and our whole way of life, not just an hour or two in the morning when we sit in silent contemplative prayer. For most of us, trained for active ministry, this will probably be something quite new to us and will require that we make considerable changes in our way of thinking and living.

Basically, we must do with our whole life what we do in a very intense but brief way in our contemplative prayer: namely, cutting off many of the external stimuli that come to us from the world around us; that is, distractions, pleasures, diversions, entertainments, etc., for all of these churn us up, excite us, and disperse our limited affective and intellectual energies and concentration. This ends up dividing our emotions, our mind, and our heart away from the one thing necessary, which is the love of God with an undivided heart, with all our heart.

By living in this new way, cutting off many of these external stimuli, we will find ourselves better disposed when God chooses to visit us with his heavenly light and peace. Living in this new way will better enable us to enter into contemplative peace and silence, with our eyes closed and our minds and hearts focused on God.

Contemplative living, then, means living a simple, plain, sober, unadorned, recollected, and reflective life, in much silence and solitude, far from the commotion, noise, distraction, and superficiality of the world, eating simple, basic, healthy, unadorned food, and, in general, renouncing the pleasures of this world.

This then is what is meant by a life of *religious* retirement. It means that we are now retired from an active life and an active job in the world, but it is not retirement for the sake of devoting ourselves to fun and games, pleasure, fine dining, television, movies, and entertainment. That is the secular model of retirement, the worldly model. A life of *religious* retirement has, I think, little in common with the secular model of retirement, except that we no longer have to work for a living. And so we are now finally free; not free, though, to devote ourselves to a life of pleasure, but rather finally free to fully devote ourselves to God in prayer, meditation, spiritual reading, study, writing, and contemplation.

To be successful as contemplatives, we need to focus not only on how we pray, but also on how we *live*. We must pray contemplatively, but we must also *live* contemplatively. Our contemplative living forms the context within which we can begin to pray contemplatively. We must cut off distractions and images in our contemplative prayer, but we must do the same thing in our whole way of *living* if we want to live contemplatively, which is the necessary context for praying contemplatively.

The whole first book of St. John of the Cross's *Ascent of Mt Carmel*—which I highly recommend as a basic text on contemplative living—is all about the renunciation of worldly pleasures as the fundamental basis for contemplative living and union with God in contemplative praying.

This is why monks live the way they do: within a cloister or enclosure, keeping out the noise, superficiality, and distractions of the world. The monastic life is contemplative living, a life without television, movies, or much talking; a life of silence, simple, meatless meals, and much fasting.

II

THE LIFE OF RELIGIOUS RETIREMENT

Since we are now retired, we have a place to live, food to eat, no longer have to work for a living, and are free from all other obligations. This means that we now have a unique and ideal opportunity to serve God in a still more radical and even higher and more perfect way than we did before, even as active priests and brothers. And since we are celibate, we can live this life of religious retirement in an even more radical way, retiring at last from the world, finally to serve God with all our heart, with an undivided heart, serving him alone as our only Lord, for it is impossible to serve two masters (Mt 6:24), though most try.

This second master, whom most still try to serve along with God, may take many forms, from the delights of the table to addiction to television, movies, or other games or entertainments that divide the heart away from a single-minded pursuit of God.

A life of religious retirement, therefore, is not just a *retired* life in the secular sense. It is rather a *religiously* retired life, or a life of *religious* retirement, or retirement from all else for the sake of religion, for the sake of God. It is, therefore, an ascetical life, a life of renunciation, sacrifice, and voluntary poverty—a life of evangelical poverty, lived in simplicity, plainness, sobriety, and austerity, for the love of God. It is a life which recognizes that the ascetical way is the way that leads to mystical experience, to the deep, personal experience of the love of God in the heart, in an overwhelming and luminous way. The life of religious retirement is, in short, a life that has taken the ascetical-mystical path, the path of traditional spirituality.

A life of religious retirement is a life that retires from the world for the sake of God. It is a life in which we lose our life in this world, to find it truly in God (Mk 8:35). It is a life in which we hate our life in this world, to find it in God (Jn 12:25), for "He who loves his life loses it," Jesus says, "and he who hates his life in this world will keep it for eternal life" (Jn 12:25).

The one who loves his life is the one who follows the secular model of retirement, dedicating himself to a life of pleasure and, in general, imbibing the whole secular message of the ideal of a pleasure-centered life. This is loving our life. And "He who loves his life loses it," Jesus tells us (Jn 12:25).

But "he who hates his life in this world," Jesus says, "will keep it for eternal life" (Jn 12:25). The one who hates his life in this world is the one who embraces the cross and renounces the world, the one whose only pleasure is God, to the degree that this is possible. Such a one loves simplicity and plainness, "For whoever would save his life will lose it," Jesus says; "and whoever loses his life for my sake and the gospel's will save it" (Mk 8:35).

The one who would save his life is the one who seeks to fill himself with the pleasures and delicacies of this world. In reality, though, he is not saving his life at all, but rather losing it, because he is moving in the wrong direction, seeking happiness in deceitful mirages, in things that look good but that do not really give us happiness in the heart. He loses his life because he divides his heart and disperses his affective energy away from a pure and undivided love of God, the only source of happiness. Having divided his heart from the pure love of God by seeking his joy in worldly pleasures, he loses his life in the deeper sense, in the only sense that really matters. Blessed, therefore, is "every one who has left houses or brothers or sisters or father or mother or children or lands, for my name's sake," Jesus says, for he "will receive a hundredfold" (Mt 19:29).

But "whoever loses his life for my sake and the gospel's will save it" (Mk 8:35). The one who loses his life is the one who renounces the world and its pleasures for the sake of Christ, the one who embraces a life of evangelical poverty and simple living, abandoning worldly ways, styles, and customs, to live for God alone with all his heart, with an undivided heart. He, indeed, is the one who will save his life and become a true contemplative.

This is the ascetical-mystical path of spirituality and contemplative living. Such a path leads to a deep personal experience of the love of God in the heart. Yet it is a path not well-known or well-trod. Most pass it by. Few really chose it, even though it is the path of life. But did not Jesus say,

> Enter by the narrow gate; for the gate is wide and the way is easy, that leads to destruction, and those who enter by it are many. For the gate is narrow and the way is hard, that leads to life, and those who find it are few (Mt 7:13–14).

How many take the wide and easy way? Most, I think, for that is what Jesus says, namely, that it is the way of the many, not of the few. "…those who enter by it are many" (Mt 7:13). But it does not have to be that way, at least not for us. We can be among the few who do not take the easy way that leads to destruction, if only we can learn and begin to put into practice the basic principles of contemplative living, of the ascetical-mystical life, the life of religious retirement. It is a life lived wholly and radically for the Lord, renouncing the styles, delights, delicacies, entertainments, and diversions of this world. The way of the ascetical-mystical life is the way of the few, but it is, nonetheless, the way of life. It is narrow and hard. It is a life of constant prayer and fasting, but it is the only way of life. "For the gate is narrow and the way is hard, that leads to life, and those who find it are *few*" (Mt 7:14). May we be among those few.

Jesus also taught us, saying,

> The kingdom of heaven is like treasure hidden in a field,
> which a man found and covered up; then in his joy he goes
> and sells all that he has and buys that field (Mt 13:44).

What is the point of this parable? What is the treasure? It is the Kingdom of God, the light of Christ, shining in our heart. Is that not what we want? Is that not what the contemplative is seeking, namely, Christ shining resplendent in his heart, illuminating him from within with a light not of this world (2 Cor 4:6) and with a heavenly peace and experience of spiritual love that transforms him? Yes, the treasure is the Kingdom of God and the experience of contemplation. But how do we get it?

The parable teaches us how to get it. It is to sell all that we have. But what does that mean? It means living a plain, simple, unadorned, quiet life. It means losing our life in this world to find life truly in God. It means hating our life in this world to find our life in God (Jn 12:25). In short, it means renouncing the pleasures of this world and embracing the spirit of evangelical poverty, to live only for God, that he be our only pleasure in this world, to the degree that this is possible. The one who does this, who makes these renunciations, is able to buy the field and obtain the treasure.

But how many do this? Few, I think, as Jesus says, "For the gate is narrow and the way is hard that leads to life, and those who find it are *few*" (Mt 7:14). But let us be among those few! Let us be among those who choose the ascetical-mystical way of life, the way of traditional spirituality, the contemplative path, the path of contemplative living, the path of religious retirement.

III

THE EXPERIENCE OF CONTEMPLATION

What does the actual experience of contemplation do to us? It changes and transforms us. It kills our interest in the pleasures of this world, because at last we see and deeply experience where true beauty and happiness really lie. The pleasures of this world, then, seem very slight indeed in comparison with the deep inner happiness that we are now experiencing in contemplation.

Finally, the contemplative experience enables us to realize that it is precisely the pleasures of this world that choke and extinguish the flame of the love of God burning in our heart. Worldly pleasures, therefore, are seen as something to be avoided by those who love contemplation; they drown out the subtle light of contemplation and drive it from our heart, since they fill our heart with alien and deceptive images and stimuli so that we can no longer perceive the subtle beauty of contemplation.

Through contemplative experience, we finally realize that the subtle beauty of contemplation is to be sought by taking the narrow and hard way of life, the way of renunciation of the world, the way of silence and simplicity, of plainness, sobriety, and austerity. And concerning prayer, after all good and necessary reading, reflection, and meditation have ceased, we find the greatest beauty in silent, wordless, thoughtless union with God, when he shines his heavenly light, love, and supernatural peace into our heart. When this happens, we know that this indeed is the way of life.

We are, I believe, in an ideal situation at this point of our life to live a contemplative life, for we are now free at last from all other obligations, free for God.

IV

ON THE PRACTICAL SIDE

On the practical side, how precisely should we practice contemplative prayer? How precisely should we dispose ourselves for the experience of contemplative prayer when God chooses to grant it? Contemplative prayer is not something we can produce ourselves. It is a gift from God, completely above our natural powers to produce at will; but we can and should dispose and prepare ourselves for it, so that we will be ready, with our receivers turned on and tuned in, so to speak, when God chooses to give it.

We attune ourselves for contemplation by general ascetical-contemplative living, as described above; and then, in terms of actual prayer, by sitting in silence in a comfortable position in a dimly lit room with our eyes closed and our chin near our chest, so that we are not exercising any effort, even to keep our head upright. Then, I would recommend repeating the Jesus prayer, or something similar, coordinating it with your breathing, saying the first part as you inhale, and the final part, namely, "have mercy on me, a sinner," as you exhale. Do this in the beginning, with your mouth open and using your lips and tongue, but silently. Then, after you are into the rhythm of it, you can close your mouth, stop your tongue, and repeat it mentally.

I personally do this in a dimly lit room for the first half hour of the day, after dressing in the morning. I then say the office of readings and intersperse it with more silent prayer. This is usually a simple, peaceful time with the Lord, a good preparation for what follows. I then write my sermon for the day and celebrate Mass, after which I say lauds. I then sit again for another fifty minutes of silent prayer.

This final sitting is when the Lord most often visits me with love, light, and peace, and fills me with deep, refreshing, spiritual joy. But I consider the earlier sitting a necessary preparation for this final fifty minutes after receiving Holy Communion. Then, in the evening, after vespers, I sit for another fifteen minutes of silent prayer.

You who have had an active ministry but are now retired, have, I believe, a marvelous opportunity at last to begin something new and of the very greatest importance, even more important than your previous ministry.

And what could be more important before God than your active Christian ministry? Leaving the world to live a life of religious retirement, totally dedicating yourselves to the Lord in a most radical way, with all your heart in every aspect of your life. Such a life, then, forms the context within which you can experience the love of God in your heart, illuminating you from within (2 Cor 4:6), while you reflect light and peace to everyone about you.

If we can no longer do active ministry, a life of religious retirement is, I believe, the only really suitable and worthy option we have if we want to live the final years of our life in a deeply meaningful and spiritual way. I say this because the only other option is the secular model of retirement, namely, a life of fun and games, movies, television, and fine dining, a life devoted to pleasure and entertainment. Such a life is basically unworthy of us as priests and brothers. It is hardly what God would have us do with this final and most important phase of our life.

Yet even as contemplatives, if we can write, for example, or have some other skill that we can still exercise, we will still have a way of actively preaching the good news of salvation in Jesus Christ for the transformation and enlightenment of the world. This we can combine in a most felicitous way with our contemplative living and praying.

CELIBACY, AN UNDIVIDED LOVE OF GOD

"For I am jealous over you with godly jealousy: for I have espoused you to one husband, that I may present you as a chaste virgin to Christ" (2 Cor 11:2 KJV).

We see in this verse that we have a nuptial relationship with Jesus Christ. St. Paul says he has espoused us to only "one husband," who is Jesus Christ. And so we are "as a chaste virgin" presented to Christ (2 Cor 11:2). We see from this scripture that this is the ideal—namely, that our relationship with Christ should be nuptial and exclusive, as exclusive as we can possibly make it in keeping with the responsibilities of our state in life. Married people will have an exclusive relationship with Christ in keeping with their state in life as married people; but those who are celibate for the Kingdom of God—that is, those who have consecrated themselves to God as religious or consecrated persons—can have a nuptial relationship with Christ in which Christ is literally the only spouse of their heart. For them, their nuptial relationship with Christ is even more exclusive than that of married people.

Every Christian should have Jesus Christ as the only spouse of his heart with whom he has an intimate and exclusive relationship, and he should always guard his heart lest it become divided. Married people do this together as a couple, as one flesh, with Christ uniting himself with them in their marriage. Celibates do this in their own way with a radically undivided heart, not even divided by the love of a Christian spouse in the sacrament of matrimony. Celibacy is for this reason a state in life more radical than marriage because of the greater exclusivity of its nuptial bond with Christ, as literally the only spouse of the heart. Celibates can, therefore, literally love Jesus Christ with *all* their heart, with *all* the affective energy of their heart going only to him, without any division whatsoever, with a completely undivided heart.

St. Paul therefore describes the celibate vocation as follows: "The unmarried man is anxious about the affairs of the Lord, how to please the Lord; but the married man is anxious about worldly affairs, how to please his wife, and he is divided. And the unmarried woman or virgin is anxious about the affairs of the Lord, how to be holy in body and spirit; but the married woman is anxious about worldly affairs, how to please her husband" (1 Cor 7:32–34). St. Paul emphasizes the greater exclusivity of the celibate's relationship with Christ.

It is for this reason that the Church has always taught—and still does teach (see the Appendix)—that celibacy is a higher vocation than marriage. The rejection of this teaching by many today in Western Europe and the United States is one of the reasons why religious life is dying in these countries, for if one no longer believes that celibacy enables one to have a more exclusive nuptial relationship with Christ, he lacks one of the most important motives for choosing this difficult way of life.

ST. JOHN OF THE CROSS, DOCTOR OF THE ASCETICAL-MYSTICAL LIFE

St. John of the Cross has taught us much about the inner life of the soul in its journey towards union with God. In his book, *The Ascent of Mount Carmel,* he teaches us about the *active* purifications of the senses and of the spirit necessary to come into union with God. The senses of tasting, smelling, hearing, seeing, and touching must be purified of their appetites for worldly pleasure. This takes place through the mortification of the five senses. In the first book of *The Ascent of Mount Carmel,* St. John of the Cross gives many explanations and illustrations of the importance of this mortification of the five senses from the pleasures of the world.

Then in books two and three of *The Ascent of Mount Carmel,* he teaches that it is also necessary for us to *actively* purify our *spirit* from its appetites for the pleasures of this world. This means that our thoughts of these things must be purified, as well as our memory of them (including our imaginations about them), and our inner desire for them (our will). This then constitutes the purification of the three faculties of our spirit from the appetites and pleasures of this world—namely, the intellect, the memory (which includes the imagination), and the will. These three faculties of our spirit must be purified of their worldly appetites if we are to arrive at union with God in supernatural, infused contemplation.

St. John of the Cross teaches in the second and third books of *The Ascent of Mount Carmel* that it is the three theological virtues of faith, hope, and charity that purify and renew the three faculties of our spirit: faith purifies our intellect, hope purifies our memory, and charity purifies our will, which is the faculty with which we love. St. John of the Cross is unique in the tradition up to his time in the emphasis which he puts on this point. But it is through this process, according to his system, that our spirit is made godlike, namely, through the working of the three supernatural theological virtues on the three faculties of our spirit.

These, then, are the *active* purifications of the senses and of the spirit, in which we must be active in the work of purification through a life of asceticism and mortification. They are called active purifications because we ourselves must actively play a dominant role in this purification process through our own self-mortification.

There remain the *passive* purifications in which God plays the dominant role in further purifying us, and in which we remain passive. Hence they are called *passive* because we remain largely passive in them, while God is one who is active. St. John of the Cross speaks of these passive purifications in his book *The Dark Night*.

All this purification is directed towards the end of being able to contemplate God supernaturally in infused, wordless, imageless prayer in ecstatic, mystical experience, and so come into union with God. This union should eventually lead us to a new, stable, peaceful state, which St. John of the Cross calls Mystical Marriage or Spiritual Marriage.

A Monastic Reflection on Saint John of the Cross

The monastic life is a life of prayer and fasting, of work and love, of reading and obedience, of humility and silence. It is lived in the solitude of the desert, far removed from the world and its distractions, noise, and temptations, in answer to a call from God to live for him *alone,* with all the love of our heart. One may live this way in solitude or in a silent community of solitaries. One lives this way in order to purify the five senses and the three faculties of the spirit (the intellect, the memory [including the imagination], and the will) from the pleasures of the world, to the degree that this is possible in this life. This is done to become freed from the passions, so that we might arrive at a new, profound, experienced, peaceful state of union with God. It normally takes years of ascetical living to become sufficiently purified to arrive at this new stable state of peace and light in which we reflect the glory and love of God upon the world, thus raising the general spiritual level of all, loving our neighbor as ourselves (Mk 12:31).

On the way to this new state of light and peace—and while in it—we may begin at some point to experience what St. Teresa of Avila calls the "prayer of union," a profound experience of light and love, of short duration, in which the senses and faculties are suspended. It is a state that resembles sleep, but is not sleep, and during it we experience, in the darkness and unknowing of our intellect, the dazzling light of God. This light fills our whole being, illuminating us from within with divinity, satiating us with the love of God.

When we come to our normal senses again, we are convinced that we were one with God but do not know what happened to us or how it came about. We do know, though, that it was *not our own insights or meditations* that put us into that state of union, because we were not meditating on anything when we went into it; rather, it was caused by a revelation and visitation of God, which came over us and submerged us in divine light and love. This is wordless, thoughtless, imageless prayer—apophatic prayer, as we sometimes call it—although we may use an ejaculation, such as the Jesus prayer, constantly repeated, to prepare ourselves to enter into this prayer of union, for the ejaculation reduces distractions and focuses us on God.

This prayer of union, or apophatic prayer (meaning "without words"), begins to be more and more regularly experienced as we continue to live an ascetical life, purifying ourselves of our passions by denying ourselves worldly pleasures, which feed the passions, desires, and appetites, keeping them alive in us. This apophatic prayer helps us and motivates us to live *still more* ascetically; for we understand that it was our ascetical living that prepared us to be able to perceive and experience this prayer of union, which has now become more important to us than anything else in the world.

Therefore, while ascetical living disposed us to experience the prayer of union in the first place, the prayer of union now motivates us to continue living ascetically in the future in order to experience this prayer more often. Thus the prayer of union helps us to free ourselves from our passions by motivating us to deprive ourselves of the worldly pleasures that feed the passions and keep them alive in us.

We thus continue growing spiritually until we reach the goal, which is a new stable state of tranquility, peace, and love. It resembles marriage in its stability and intimate joy and fruition, and St. John of the Cross calls it mystical marriage. In this final state, for having deprived ourselves of the pleasures of this world, we are rewarded with the deepest gifts of light, love, and peace.

We do not always experience this peace, love, and light to the same degree. In fact, most of the time it is barely perceptible, but we know that it is there, and we are happy and deeply at peace because of it (*The Living Flame of Love* 4.14.4). But then there are many times when this peace and light awaken within us and become very intense for many hours, for a whole morning, or a whole day, or even for several days without interruption. And then, afterward, it is as though it falls gently back to sleep again within us, and we remain consoled by its gentle, loving, sleeping presence (*Flame* 4.14.4).

The monastic life is set up to provide an optimal setting within which we can follow this trajectory and live a deeply spiritual life. We begin by living ascetically, and eventually we move into mystical experience. Yet we never abandon our ascetical living, for if we do, our passions will reawaken, and we will go backward. We begin by living in silence and solitude—although not total silence and solitude—and by guarding all our senses, depriving them of their pleasurable objects, especially the senses of taste, sight, and hearing.

We eat the plainest, simplest food to mortify our sense of taste from pleasure. In the days of St. Bernard, for example, his monks ate food seasoned *only* with salt, nothing fried, no meat, and nothing made of white flour, not even white bread, which gives greater pleasure at the expense of nutrition. They ate only whole grains and no delicacies (see his *First Letter* #11–12; 20). They also ate only one meal a day for six months of the year, never eating anything before noon and only eating in the evening from Easter until September 14. In the times and places of greatest monastic fervor, we find many examples of this sort.

Monks mortify their sight by living within a cloister and by practicing strict custody of the eyes while in choir in the church. They do not usually even see the guests, who remain in the guesthouse. They also mortify sight, hearing, and taste by remaining within the cloister and not taking trips, except to the doctor, and not going out to eat in restaurants. Finally they mortify their sense of hearing by not listening to the radio, television, or secular music.

In time, we will become purified, not only in our five senses, but also in the three faculties of our spirit (intellect, memory, and will), so that the desire for the pleasures which we deprive our senses of gradually dries up within us, and we less and less think of them (the intellect), remember or imagine them (the memory, including the imagination), or long for them (the will). The more purified we become from the pleasures of the world, the more we are freed from our passions, which become increasingly dormant within us. If we stop living ascetically, they will reawaken. Hence ascetical living is *constantly* practiced for the *whole* of life.

This is *our* part. At the same time, God is also acting within us, doing *his* part; and when he sees us renouncing the pleasures of the world and seeking him in prayer, he steps in and helps us, further drying up our passions. One of the ways he does this is by allowing us to feel guilty for not living ascetically, when at times we fall into imperfections—for example, breaking silence, or communicating at times or in places of silence with signs or gestures, or not guarding our sight (looking at the bulletin board during the time of the great monastic silence during the night, etc.).

These times of guilt feelings are something new to us. In our former life, we never felt guilty or depressed about such things. That is because we were not yet living ascetically, and God was not yet doing *his* part to help dry up our passions. Now, however, everything is different. Once we begin to *actively* purify our senses and spirit, God also begins to purify them.

The active purifications are what *we* do by living ascetically. Saint John of the Cross discusses our active purifications, which we do, in *The Ascent of Mount Carmel*, the first book dealing with the deprivation and purification of the five senses from worldly pleasures, and the second and third books dealing with the deprivation and purification of the three faculties of the spirit from the pleasures of this world. So here we have St. John of the Cross's great system of the active and passive purifications of the senses and of the spirit to prepare the soul for the prayer of union and mystical marriage. Monastic life is set up to provide an optimal setting where this can take place.

One must begin *by living an ascetical life*. Spiritual directors should encourage rather than discourage this. St. John of the Cross sharply criticizes directors who discourage ascetical living, because they slow souls down (*Flame* 3.62).

He also says, "the road and ascent to God, then, demands a habitual effort to renounce and mortify the appetites; the sooner this mortification is achieved, the sooner the soul reaches the top. But until the appetites are eliminated, a person will not arrive ... for he will fail to acquire perfect virtue, which is in keeping the soul empty, naked, and purified of every appetite" (*Ascent* I.5.6).

"Until a man is purged of his attachments he will not be equipped to possess God" (*Ascent* I.4.3).

"God commanded that the Ark of the Covenant be empty and hollow (Ex 27:8) to remind the soul how void of all things God wishes it, if it is to serve as his worthy dwelling" (*Ascent* I.5.7).

"Until slumber comes to the appetites through the mortification of sensuality, and until this very sensuality is stilled in such a way that the appetites do not war against the spirit, the soul will not walk out to genuine freedom, to the enjoyment of union with its Beloved" (*Ascent* I.15.2).

"It is noteworthy that God is very ready to comfort and satisfy the soul in her needs and afflictions when she neither has nor desires consolation and satisfaction outside of Him" (*The Spiritual Canticle* 10.6).

"As the soul longing to focus the eyes of her will upon the light of something outside of God is justly deprived of the divine light ... so also does the soul that closes its eyes to all things in order to open them to God alone merit congruously the illumination of the divine light" (*Sp. Cant.* 10.9).

The saint says that the two effects of mystical marriage are "forgetfulness or withdrawal from all worldly things, and mortification of all her appetites and gratifications" (*Sp. Cant.* 26.2).

"... in order not to fail God she [the soul] failed all that is not God, that is, herself and all other creatures, losing all these for love of him" (*Sp. Cant.* 29.10).

"To journey to God, the will must walk in detachment from every pleasant thing, rather than in attachment to it" (*Flame* 3.51).

"The appetite and sensory gratification impede the knowledge of high things" (*Flame* 3.73).

"He who does not allow his appetites to carry him away will soar in his spirit as swiftly as the bird that lacks no feathers" (*Sayings of Light and Love* 23).

"The perfect man rejoices in what afflicts the imperfect man" (*Sayings of Light and Love* 54). That is, he rejoices in fasting, self-denial, and mortification; in solitude and silence; in simplicity and evangelical poverty; in living within a cloister and not traveling about, for thus he comes to deep peace, and experiences God regularly in light and love.

"The less one takes of things and pleasures, the farther one advances along the way" (*Sayings of Light* 55).

"Crucified inwardly and outwardly with Christ, you will live in this life with fullness and satisfaction of soul" (*Maxims and Counsels* 8). Truly the *crucified* life is the *risen* life. Therefore, St. Paul was crucified to the world, and the world to him (Gal 6:14).

"...do not seek pleasure in any temporal thing, and your soul will concentrate on goods you know not" (*Maxims* 17).

"He who seeks not the *cross* of Christ seeks not the *glory* of Christ" (*Maxims* 23). Living the cross of Christ, mortified to the pleasures of the world, is to live a life of inner glory.

"Wisdom enters through love, silence, and mortification" (*Maxims* 30).

"The further you withdraw from earthly things the closer you approach heavenly things and the more you find in God" (*Other Counsels* 1).

"That the soul have success in journeying to God and being joined to him, it must have the mouth of its will opened only to God Himself, empty of every morsel of appetite, that God may fill it with his love and sweetness; and it must remain with this hunger and thirst for God alone, without desiring to be satisfied by any other thing" (*Letter* 12).

"He invites to the abundance of the divine waters of union with God only those who thirst for God alone and who have no other thirst, that is, other appetites" (*Letter* 12).

"...we will be unhappy with God, even though He is always with us, if our heart is not alone, but attached to something else" (*Letter* 14). The saint tells us not to forsake God, the fount, and make for ourselves leaky cisterns that do not satisfy (Jer 2:13; *Ascent* I.6.1).

In mystical marriage, "She [the soul] no longer goes about in search of her own gain or pleasures" (*Sp. Cant.* 28.2). "I no longer follow after my pleasures and appetites" (*Sp. Cant.* 28.6). In the state of mystical marriage, "He who walks in the love of God seeks neither his own gain nor his reward, but only to lose all things and himself for God; and this loss he judges to be his gain ... He who does not know how to lose himself, does not find himself, but rather loses himself" (*Sp. Cant.* 29.11).

The saint writes that "a man's intellect, clouded by the appetites, becomes dark and impedes the sun of either natural reason or supernatural wisdom from shining within and completely illumining it" (*Ascent* I.8.1).

"Oh, if men but knew what a treasure of divine light this blindness caused by their affections and appetites deprives them of" (*Ascent* I.8.6). If we want to live in the light and bask in God's splendor, we must live a gloriously crucified life, constantly crucifying and mortifying ourselves to the pleasures of this world. "...the unmortified appetites result in killing a man in his relationship with God" (*Ascent* I.10.3).

"...the chief concern of spiritual directors with their penitents is the immediate mortification of every appetite. The directors should make them remain empty of what they desire so as to liberate them from so much misery" (*Ascent* I.12.6).

St. John of the Cross describes the soul in the final state of mystical marriage, saying, "The solitude in which she lived consisted of the desire to go without the things of the world for her Bridegroom's sake ... by striving for perfection, acquiring perfect solitude in which she reaches union with the Word. She consequently attains to complete refreshment and rest, signified here by the nest which refers to repose" (*Sp. Cant.* 35.4).

We come into union with God, especially in mystical marriage, by *emptying* the three faculties of the spirit of the images, news, affections, and pleasures of the world. The saint says, "In this solitude, away from all things, the soul is alone with God, and He guides, moves, and raises her to divine things. That is: He elevates her intellect to divine understanding, because it is alone and divested of other contrary and alien knowledge; He moves her will freely to the love of God, because it is alone and freed from other affections; and he fills her memory with divine knowledge, because it is now alone and empty of other images and fantasies. Once the soul disencumbers these faculties and empties them of everything inferior and or attachment to even superior things, leaving them alone without them, God engages them in the invisible and divine" (*Sp. Cant.* 35.5).

Concerning apophatic prayer, he writes, "God infuses this love in the will when it is empty and detached from other particular earthly or heavenly pleasures and affections. Take care, then, to empty the will of its affections and detach it from them. If it does not retrogress through the desire for some satisfaction or pleasure, it advances ... And it loves him above all lovable things, since it has rejected all gratifications and pleasures of these things, and they have become distasteful to it" (*Flame* 3.51).

"To journey to God, the will must walk in detachment from every pleasant thing" (*Flame* 3.51).

"One cannot reach this union without remarkable purity, and this purity is unattainable without vigorous mortification and nakedness regarding all creatures … Whoever refuses to go out at night in search for the Beloved and to divest and mortify his will, but rather seeks the Beloved one in his own bed and comfort, as did the bride (Ct 3:1), will not succeed in finding Him" (*The Dark Night* II.24.4).

Concerning apophatic prayer, the saint writes that one "should learn to remain in God's presence with a loving attention and a tranquil intellect, even though he seems to himself to be idle. For little by little and very soon the divine calm and peace, with a wondrous, sublime knowledge of God, enveloped in divine love, will be infused into his soul" (*Ascent* II.15.5).

Apophatic prayer knows by *unknowing* because "God transcends the intellect and is incomprehensible and inaccessible to it. Hence while the intellect is understanding, it is not approaching God but withdrawing from Him. It must withdraw from itself and from its knowledge so as to journey to God in faith, by believing and not understanding" (*Flame* 3.48).

God dwells differently in different souls. In those who renounce all for him, he dwells as their master, and they experience him profoundly. They even experience him when it seems like he is asleep within them (*Flame* 4.14). But in those who do *not* purify themselves from the pleasures of the world, God dwells in them as a stranger and they experience *very* little of him (*Flame* 4.16). "It is in the soul in which less of its own appetites and pleasures dwell where he [God] dwells more alone, more pleased … the Beloved dwells secretly with an embrace so much the closer, more intimate, and interior, the purer and more alone the soul is to everything other than God" (*Flame* 4.14).

But why are there so few who reach these heights? It is because few are willing to endure such an ascetical and mortified life. Few are willing to renounce the pleasures of the world (*Flame* 2.27). St. John of the Cross writes that "the reason is not because God wishes that there be only a few of these spirits so elevated; He would rather want all to be perfect, but he finds few vessels that will endure so lofty and sublime a work. Since He tries them in little things and finds them so weak that they immediately flee from work, unwilling to be subject to the least discomfort and mortification … He proceeds no further in purifying them…

"There are many who desire and persistently beseech God to bring them to this state of perfection. Yet when God wills to conduct them through the initial trials and mortifications, as is necessary, they are unwilling to suffer them, and they shun them, flee from the narrow road of life, and seek the broad road of their own consolation, which is that of their own perdition; thus they do not allow God to begin to grant their petition. They are like useless containers, for although they desire to reach the state of the perfect, they do not want to be guided by the path of trials which leads to it" (*Flame* 2.27).

Hence, as I said before, St. John of the Cross says that spiritual directors should encourage their penitents to live an ascetical life. The saint sharply criticizes directors who discourage ascetical living, saying, "It will happen that God is anointing some souls with the unctions of holy desires and motives for renouncing the world, changing their way of life, and serving Him, with contempt for the world—and God esteems this stage to which he has brought them, because worldly things do not please Him—when these directors, by their human rationalizations or reflections, singularly contrary to the doctrine of Christ and his humility and contempt for all things, and depending on their own interests or satisfactions, or out of fear where there is no reason to fear, either make matters difficult for these souls, or cause them to delay, or even worse try to make them put the thought from their minds.

"With a spirit not too devout, with little of Christ's meekness and fully clothed in worldliness, since they do not enter by the narrow gate of life, these directors do not let others enter either. Our Lord threatens them through St. Luke: Woe to you, for you have taken away the key to knowledge and you neither enter yourselves nor do you allow others to enter (Lk 11:52). These directors are indeed like barriers or obstacles at the gate of heaven, hindering those who seek their counsel from entering" (*Flame* 3.62).

The soul in the state of mystical marriage, at the end of the spiritual journey, by denying herself all satisfaction and pleasure in this world, has finally reached a new stable state of light, peace, love, and joy in the Lord. The saint describes her in this way: "Since she wished to live in solitude, apart from every satisfaction, comfort and support of creatures, in order to reach companionship and union with her Beloved, she deserved to discover the possession of peaceful solitude in her Beloved, in whom she rests, alone and isolated from all these disturbances ... insofar as she desired to live apart from all created things, in solitude for her Beloved's sake, He Himself was enamored of her because of this solitude and took care of her by accepting her in His arms, feeding her in Himself with every blessing, and guiding her to the high things of God" (*Sp. Cant.* 35.2).

Indeed from the beginning to the end of the spiritual life we are to seek our delight only in God, *not* in the pleasures of this world. Those who take this traditional ascetical path of the saints will be prepared to enter into a mystical life of union with God, which culminates in mystical marriage. The saint beautifully describes it in the following way, comparing the soul to the white turtledove that Noah released from the ark to see whether the waters had subsided.

"...she [the soul] must advance with such love and solicitude as not to set the foot of her appetite on the green branch of any delight, or drink the clear water of any worldly honor and glory, nor should she desire the taste of the cool water of any temporal refreshment or comfort, or to settle in the shade of any creature's favor and protection, nor should she desire in any way to rest in anything or to have the company of other affections, but she should always sigh for solitude in all things until she reaches her Bridegroom in complete satisfaction" (*Sp. Cant.* 34.5).

Because she lived a life so detached from the pleasures of this world, she has now reached a new state of deep rest in God, the state of mystical marriage, which the saint describes as follows: "Because the soul, before reaching this high state, went about with deep love in search of her Beloved and was satisfied with nothing else than Him ... now the turtledove has found her longed-for mate by the green river banks. This is similar to saying: Now the bride alights on the green branch, delighting in her Beloved; now she drinks the clear water of sublime contemplation and wisdom of God, and the cool water of her refreshment and comfort in God; and she also rests in the shade of His protection and favor—which she so longed for—where she is divinely and delightfully consoled, fed, and refreshed" (*Sp. Cant.* 34.6). Because she renounced every human satisfaction, comfort, and pleasure, she now finds every satisfaction, comfort, and delight in God.

This is indeed the ideal and the itinerary of the spiritual life; and monastic life—with its silence, solitude, prayer, cloister, fasting, austerity, and asceticism—is set up to provide one with an optimal environment for following this itinerary and arriving at this new state of rest, peace, and light in the Lord.

So all you who desire this wisdom, come and follow this path in wisdom's service, "For in her service you will toil a little while, and soon you will eat of her produce. She seems very harsh to the uninstructed; a weakling will not remain with her. She will weigh him down like a heavy testing stone, and he will not be slow to cast her off. For wisdom is like her name, and is not manifest to many ... [But] at last you will find the rest she gives, and she will be changed into joy for you. Then her fetters will become for you a strong protection, and her collar a glorious robe. Her yoke is a golden ornament, and her bonds are a cord of blue. You will wear her like a glorious robe, and put her on like a crown of gladness" (Sirach 6:19–22,28–31).

Monks live this way because, although the world reveals the goodness of God, God is infinitely greater than the revelation of his goodness in creation, and those who wish to come into profound union with him must seek him in himself, beyond the good things created by him.

THE IMPORTANCE OF THE ASCETICAL DIMENSION IN CHRISTIAN SPIRITUALITY

The world, as God's creation, is full of good and necessary things that we need to sustain life and promote the Kingdom of God, things that we use in his service and for his glory. The first part of the spiritual journey builds on the good things of this world that reveal to us the goodness of God. But the great mystical writers also teach *renunciation* of the world in order to reach a deeper mystical union with God and a state of tranquility, light, and peace. This is the *ascetical-mystical* path of contemplative living, which is a more advanced path but nonetheless meant for all, as Vatican II has taught us. If only there were more who knew this path and could teach it to the people of God.

Once one has gone a certain way, seeing God in all things, in the good things of his creation, the way to go further is the apophatic, ascetical-mystical path—the path of renunciation and silence, the path of silent mystical prayer—which will take us to the *top* of this mountain. This is traditional spirituality. What is needed, therefore, is for those who know this tradition to present these basic principles of traditional monastic wisdom to the whole people of God. The basic spiritual principles are the same for all; but they will be applied differently, adapted to the vocation and state of life of each one. What monks have traditionally lived in a very literal and radical way can be lived by all of God's people, each in the way that the Holy Spirit will guide him.

The monastic tradition of asceticism and renunciation of the world is clearly *not* to be understood as a depreciation of the world, of the body, or of creation. It is *not* in any way based on a dualistic view of the world, considering matter evil and only the spirit good.

The reason for the renunciation, asceticism, and austerity, which one finds everywhere in the monastic tradition, is based rather on the desire to renounce the good for the sake of the better. That is, the ascetic and monastic tradition renounces the goods of *this* world for those of the Kingdom of God; it renounces the goods of *this* creation for those of the *new* creation. The reason for this renunciation is to have a heart completely undivided, reserved for the Lord alone.

I believe that what is needed today is a balanced view of the spiritual and contemplative life, one that is *both* ascetical and mystical, *both* cataphatic (seeing God in creation and in vocal prayer) and apophatic (experiencing God through renunciation and silent prayer). Asceticism is the path that leads to mysticism. And a cataphatic approach to life, which sees God in everything and prays using words and images, is the first part of the spiritual journey, which is to end in the apophatic experience of God without words, images, or ideas, and in detachment from the delights of this world. Renouncing the unnecessary pleasures of this world is the way to have a heart undivided and reserved for the Lord alone, and hence to be more prepared to *experience* him in inner light and glory.

Nowadays, it is at times questioned whether we really need asceticism and detachment from the pleasures of this world in order to enter into union with God and arrive at a state of peace and light in the Lord, interspersed with the luminous experience of apophatic prayer. In light of this doubt, it would be helpful, I believe, to see that this is indeed the teaching of the most standard and approved spiritual authors, such as St. Bernard, St. John Cassian, St. John of the Cross, and *The Imitation of Christ*.

One spiritual author writes thus: "The renunciation of the world and its false joys, the negation of oneself, the depreciation of the sensible, etc. are not an absurd annihilation of the human person, but rather the providential condition for attaining the full liberation and highest development of the personality; we detach ourselves from all and even from ourselves in order to fill ourselves with God and be dominated entirely by love" (Marchetti-Salvatori, 1.565–567).

St. John of the Cross writes: "there are few souls which allow themselves to be purified and detached in their depths by the Lord, and therefore there are few saints" (*The Living Flame of Love* B 2.27).

The Imitation of Christ says: "The more you retire from the consolations of all creatures, so much the sweeter and more blessed will be the consolations you will receive from your Creator" (3.12).

St. John of the Cross also says: "The soul which puts its fondness in creatures will not be able to comprehend God" (*Ascent of Mount Carmel* 1.4.3), and "the soul which puts its heart in the goods of the world, is supremely evil before God. And thus, as evil cannot comprehend the good, in the same way such a soul cannot unite itself to God" (*Ascent* 1.4.4.).

St. John of the Cross also writes: "the soul which is to ascend this mount of perfection and communicate with God, not only has to renounce all things and leave them below, but also the appetites ... And thus it is necessary that the road and ascent to God be a regular care to make cease and to mortify the appetites; and so much the quicker will the soul arrive the more diligently it gives itself to this" (*Ascent* 1.5.6). And, "Until the appetites become dormant through the mortification of our sensuality, and until our sensuality itself becomes quieted, so that there be no war within the spirit, the soul will not depart in true freedom to enjoy union with its beloved" (*Ascent* 1.15.2).

St. Anthony of Egypt said, "The intelligence of the soul becomes strong when the pleasures of the body become weak" (St. Athanasius, *Life of St. Anthony* 7). This is also the teaching of St. Bernard. His *First Letter* and his third and fourth sermons for Christmas are good examples of the emphasis that he places on the importance of an austere life. He says, "For him who lives with prudence and sobriety, salt is sufficient, and his only seasoning is hunger (*Letter* 1.11). And, "*flee delight*, because *death* is posted at the threshold of *delight*. Do penitence and you will approach the kingdom" (*Third Sermon for Christmas* #3). The reason for this renunciation is to have an undivided heart in our love and devotion to the Lord.

The Imitation of Christ is especially rich in this doctrine. Here are a few examples of it on this point: "When a man arrives at that point of perfection in which he seeks his consolation in no created thing, then God begins for the first time to be sweet for him" (1.25). "A man approaches God all the more when he separates himself from all earthly pleasure" (3.42.2). "Son, my grace is precious, and it does not want to be mixed with extraneous things, nor with earthly consolations" (3.53.1). "We are at fault if we do not taste—or only very rarely—divine consolations, because we do not seek contrition of heart, nor do we reject vain and exterior joys" (1.21.3). "If you wish to have true joy and be consoled by me abundantly, put your happiness in the depreciation of all the things of the world, and in cutting off all earthly delight. In this way you will enjoy great consolation" (3.12.4). "If you leave off being consoled by worldly things, you will be able to see more perfectly heavenly things" (2.1). And, "true glory and holy joy is ... not to delight oneself in any creature, but rather only in You" (3.40.5).

Once again, the reason for this renunciation of the world and its pleasures is to have a heart reserved uniquely for the Lord, an *undivided heart*.

Apophatic Living
as the Context
for Apophatic
Praying

The eremitic life seeks personally experienced union with God through silence, solitude, fasting, and prayer. The prayer is both cataphatic (vocal) and apophatic (wordless), but with the emphasis on the higher apophatic type. The eremitic way of life seeks depth in apophatic prayer through apophatic living, which means finding God in renunciation of the pleasures of this world. While we see God in all the things of his good creation, the more advanced path taught by the mystics is to seek him via the renunciation of the pleasures of this world, in order to have an undivided heart to be able to experience him more profoundly. Thus the beginning of the spiritual journey makes use of the cataphatic path of seeing God in the good things of his good creation and in vocal prayer; but the end of this journey is to come into deep union with God through the more advanced apophatic path of finding God in renunciation of the unnecessary pleasures of this world and in wordless mystical prayer.

Many today are interested in contemplative, apophatic prayer, sometimes called centering prayer; but not all are interested in pursuing it within the context of apophatic living, which is the life of silence, solitude, fasting, and renunciation of the pleasures of this world. Yet it is only by pursuing apophatic prayer within the context of apophatic living that we can have the deepest success in arriving at union with God and growth in mystical prayer.

Apophatic living is ascetical living. It leads to deep, apophatic, mystical prayer and experience of God's love. Thus the apophatic or ascetic way of life, which is the eremitic life, leads to apophatic or mystical prayer. The ascetical path is the path that leads us to mysticism. The eremitic life of prayer and fasting in the desert is the ascetical path, which leads to deep mystical prayer.

Apophatic or ascetic or eremitic living leads to apophatic mystical prayer and union with God. Those who seek to practice contemplative prayer, centering prayer, apophatic prayer, mystical prayer, the prayer of silence, or the prayer of union—all different names for the same thing—should do so within the context of apophatic living.

HEALTHY FASTING

"Now John's disciples and the Pharisees were fasting; and people came and said to him, Why do John's disciples and the disciples of the Pharisees fast, but your disciples do not fast? And Jesus said to them, Can the wedding guests fast while the bridegroom is with them? As long as they have the bridegroom with them, they cannot fast. The days will come, when the bridegroom is taken away from them, and then they will fast in that day" (Mk 2:18–20).

The time of the earthly ministry of Jesus Christ was a special and exceptional time in the history of salvation, and therefore his disciples did not fast during that time. But after his death and resurrection, his disciples did fast, as did those of John and of the Pharisees. The Jews fasted twice a week (Lk 18:2), on Mondays and Thursdays, while Christians fasted on Wednesdays and Fridays (Didache 8:1).

The reason for fasting is to help us to have an undivided heart in our love of God. It is easy to divide our heart among the delights of this world and among the delicacies of the table, and so our interest and love and pleasure come from many sources, and not only from God; and so we do not love God with all our heart, with a heart not divided between God on the one hand, and the delights of the world and of the table on the other hand.

Thus, for example, the desert fathers and monks in the days of St. Bernard fasted by renouncing delicacies, seasoning (except salt), and meat. Such abstinence is a form of fasting, and it does not harm one's health. Thus, following this form, we can eat all that is necessary for health, and as much quantity as we need, but at the same time renounce the addition of delicacies and seasoning, which are only added for pleasure; and in this way we can focus ourselves better only on God, with an undivided heart as our only source of pleasure, to the degree that this is possible. And so our happiness in God normally increases.

Another form of fasting is to eliminate one or two meals daily, and thus, for example, eat only once a day, a practice which was common among the desert fathers and among monks. This too is a renunciation of pleasure, so that God alone be the only pleasure of our life. But this form of fasting has the advantage of also disposing us well physically for prayer, contemplation, and various spiritual exercises, such as *lectio divina*, spiritual reading, study, and writing during the morning. This is so because if we eat only at midday, our digestion will be completed when we pray very early in the morning, and monks usually begin their morning prayer around three in the morning. But if we eat in the evening, we will still be weighed down with food at three in the morning; and if we eat again in the morning, we drop ourselves spiritually by eating just when we are at our optimal time for prayer, contemplation, and spiritual exercises.

St. Anthony's Life of Religious Retirement

"If you would be perfect, go, sell what you possess and give to the poor, and you will have treasure in heaven; and come, follow me" (Mt 19:21).

St. Anthony of Egypt, one of the great founders of monastic life, chose to do what most think would make them unhappy and gave up what most think would make them happy; and yet he was the happiest man of all in the true happiness of God. He chose to live in the desert, after having renounced all that he had in this world. There, he lived an austere, ascetic life of prayer, fasting, and manual labor. "He ate once daily, after sunset, but there were times when he received food every second and frequently even every fourth day. His food was bread and salt, and for drinking he took only water" (*Life* 7). He said, "the soul's intensity is strong when the pleasures of the body are weakened" (*Life* 7). His life was one of withdrawal into the solitude of the desert for contemplation.

St. Anthony is a good reminder for monks today not to forget the ascetical side of their life, and only want to remember its pleasant side. In our days, when many have renounced asceticism and austerity, especially in the area of food, it is good that the Church reminds us of St. Anthony. Eating only bread and water is probably too difficult, if not impossible, for most of us; but it is still possible to live an austere life, eating only simple, plain, and basic foods—without meat, fried foods, sugar, delicacies, fancy desserts, or seasoning, except salt—eating only vegetables boiled in water, plain fruits, whole-grain bread and whole-grain cereals, beans and legumes, cheese, and water to drink, for example. Salt is always permitted, even in the strictest monastic diets of only bread water because it is necessary for life, especially in the desert. In this way, one has an austere diet, but one that still covers all five basic food categories for health: protein (fish, eggs, cheese, beans, peanuts), cereal, vegetable, fruit, and dairy.

The reason for living an austere and ascetic life is that it purifies us to be empty for God, to come into union with him in prayer and contemplation.

When we are full of the good things of *this* creation, we forget those of the *new* creation. Hence, if we are wise, we will, like St. Anthony, renounce the pleasures of *this* life for those of the Kingdom of God.

Jesus taught us that if we want the buried treasure, which is the Kingdom of God shining within us, we have to sell all that we have (Mt 13:44), noting that this is the true path of discipleship. He said, "So therefore, whoever of you does not renounce all that he has cannot be my disciple" (Lk 14:33). We are to have only one treasure, and that in heaven, not also here on earth (Mt 6:19–21). "For where your treasure is, there will your heart be also" (Mt 6:21).

It is better to have our consolation in God than in the pleasures of this world. May Jesus not say to us, "But woe to you that are rich, for you have received your consolation" (Lk 6:24). St. Anthony chose this austere and ascetic way because he saw it as the clearest and best way to enter into and live in the Kingdom of God, for "it is easier for a camel to go through the eye of a needle," said Jesus, "than for a rich man to enter the kingdom of God" (Mt 19:24).

Fasting in Christian and Religious Life

"Then the disciples of John came to him, saying, Why do we and the Pharisees fast, but your disciples do not fast? And Jesus said to them, Can the wedding guests mourn as long as the bridegroom is with them? The days will come, when the bridegroom is taken away from them, and then they will fast" (Mt 9:14–15).

We now live in the days when the bridegroom has been physically taken from us, and therefore we now fast. Fasting is an important element in the life of every Christian, for by fasting we keep guard over our heart, that it remain undivided, reserved for the Lord alone, not divided among the many delights and delicacies of the table and of the world in general.

Fasting is also very important for monastic and religious life, and in this we may also include societies of apostolic life and all who are celibate for the Kingdom of God.

A monk or hermit is someone who lives a life of prayer and fasting in the desert, far from the world. He lives in the desert to *separate* himself from the world, with its distractions, noise, attractions, temptations, delicacies, and delights, in order to focus on God alone with all the affection of his heart. He guards his heart in the desert so that it not divide between God and the delights of this world, so that he might live a contemplative life of prayer and union with God in peace and light. A monk or hermit lives a life of stability, obedience, and conversion of ways (the three traditional monastic vows, older than the vows of present-day religious). That is, he lives for God alone, in *stability*, not traveling about for pleasure, but rather focusing his life and mind on one thing only, God, in one single place, without distraction. He *obeys* God in all that he reveals to him, and lives as God guides him in order to remain in his peace and love. And he completely converts himself from a worldly way of living (*conversion of ways*), leaving behind the world's endless quest for pleasure, in order to live in God's love, light, and peace. For the monk, fasting is an integral element of his new life. It means avoiding and

48

renouncing the delights of the table and of life in general, and rather eating and living in great simplicity, embracing evangelical poverty and the life of the cross.

Religious and those living celibacy for the Kingdom of God live a life of *poverty*, *chastity*, and *obedience* (the three present-day religious vows)— whether in formal vows or not—in order to live for God alone with all their heart, with an undivided heart, reserved for the Lord alone and the service of the Church. For them, poverty is essential for maintaining an undivided heart; they live chastely, without dividing their heart with the love of a woman; and they try to obey the will of God in every detail of their life, so as to remain in his peace. For religious, fasting is essential. They no longer live for the unnecessary pleasures of the world, but rather simply, poorly, and without worldly pleasures, eating simple, plain, healthy food, without delicacies, so as to find their pleasure in God alone, to the degree that this is possible.

THE CALL TO PERFECTION

"Jesus said to him, If you would be perfect, go, sell what you possess and give to the poor, and you will have treasure in heaven; and come, follow me" (Mt 19:21).

This is the great call to perfection. We can be perfect by renouncing all else of this world for the sake of Jesus Christ in order to follow him with all our time, energy, mind, soul, heart, and strength" (Mk 12:30). This call to perfection is directed to all (Lk 14:33; Mt 5:48), although here it is directed to this rich young man. Depending on one's state in life, one can answer this call in a more, or less radical way. In this case, this rich young man is invited literally to leave all and unite himself to the band of apostles and follow Jesus wherever he goes in order to preach the Gospel. He refused this call because he found it too difficult. In reaction, Jesus said, "it will be hard for a rich man to enter the kingdom of heaven ... it is easier for a camel to go through the eye of a needle than for a rich man to enter the kingdom of God" (Mt 19:23–24).

And what does this mean for us? If, for example, our work is writing, does this mean that we have to live without clothing, without a desk, without a chair and lamp, without books, and without a computer? I do not believe this is necessary. But what then is the meaning of this scripture for us? It is a call to perfection that few want to hear or follow. It means that we are to serve God completely. We may have all the tools necessary for our profession and work, but outside of that, we are to live a life of radical poverty. St. Maximilian Kolbe is a good example of this. He had all the proper tools of his profession as a writer, printer, and publisher. He had large machines, but he and his religious companions lived in great simplicity, eating very simply off tin plates, on a simple table, dressing in Franciscan habits. Their neighbors were shocked at the simplicity and poverty of their life.

So should our life also be if we want to live a life of perfection, a life for God alone in every aspect of our life. Truly, there are few, even among religious, who follow this call to perfection, for it is difficult, and the sacrifices required are real. It is a call to change our style of life, of dressing, of eating, and of spending our free time. Instead of spending our free time in worldly pastimes, we now use this precious time for the Lord. Instead of dressing in a worldly way, if we are priests or religious, we now dress religiously. Instead of taking pleasure trips, we practice stability and sobriety. Instead of eating delicacies, we eat simple, plain, austere food for the love of God. This is how we should respond to Jesus' call to perfection and so live for God alone with *all* our heart, mind, and soul. This is the narrow path of the *few* that leads to life, not the easy path of the *many* that leads to destruction (Mt 7:13–14). May we be among the few that choose it.

FORTY DAYS IN THE DESERT

"The Spirit immediately drove him out into the desert. And he was in the desert forty days, tempted by Satan; and he was with the wild beasts; and the angels ministered to him" (Mk 1:12–13).

Lent is a time of more intense prayer and fasting in imitation of Jesus' forty days of prayer and fasting in the desert. St. Matthew says, "And he fasted forty days and forty nights, and afterwards he was hungry" (Mt 4:2). And St. Luke says that he was "forty days in the desert … And he ate nothing in those days; and when they were ended, he was hungry" (Lk 4:2).

During Lent, we imitate Jesus during his forty day retreat in the desert. Although he ate nothing during those days—and few will imitate him in this—nonetheless, we do something along this line during Lent in order to imitate his retreat of more intense prayer and fasting in the desert, far from the world with its entertainments and distractions.

We do this in order to cleanse our heart to be able to love God with all our heart. To love God with all our heart means not putting other things into our heart in place of him or in competition with him, so that our heart be not divided between God on the one hand, and these other unnecessary things on the other hand; for if we divide our heart in this way amid the various unnecessary pleasures of the world, we will not have as much affective energy left for God. Our affective energy will be divided and dispersed in many directions, and our love for God will be weakened.

It is in order to have a love for God that is not weakened, not divided, but rather strong, that we go on an annual retreat with Jesus Christ into the desert, seeking silence and solitude, and spending time with him in prayer and contemplation. We renounce worldly entertainments and pleasures and reduce our food to the essentials, giving up delicacies and things designed only for pleasure.

For monks, their whole life is a continual Lent, and so in the days of St. Bernard, for example, they did not even use seasoning on their food, other than salt; and they did this so that the Lord alone would be their only pleasure. We can follow their example if we want to live a contemplative life, dedicating ourselves to contemplation. But during Lent at least, all Christians will do something along this line.

The preface for the First Sunday of Lent says Christ's "fast of forty days makes this a holy season of self-denial." And the fourth preface of Lent says, "with bodily fasting you restrain our passions, elevate our spirit, and strengthen and reward us."

Fasting can take many forms. Cistercian and Carthusian monks and most Orthodox monks, for example, seldom or never eat meat. Some eat nothing but whole wheat bread, salt, and water on certain days; others, such as St. Bernard's monks, gave up seasoning, except salt. You can renounce delicacies and things made of white flour and sugar, things which have nothing to do with health but only with pleasure, a pleasure that divides the heart from an undivided love of God alone. You can eat only twice a day or but once a day, at midday, to be light in the early morning and ready for prayer, contemplation, *lectio divina*, spiritual reading, and the silent, meditative work of the morning.

If you eat only at noon, your digestion will be completed when you begin your prayer very early in the morning. But it is difficult to complete the digestion of a big supper before rising early for prayer—and monks rise about three in the morning! Breakfast, furthermore, will drop you spiritually right in the middle of your optimal time for contemplation and the silent, meditative work of the morning. This is why eating but once a day at noon is a common practice in the monastic tradition.

Fasting is therefore an essential element of the contemplative life, which is a life exclusively dedicated to God as our only love and only pleasure.

Moses and Elijah are our models from the Old Testament during the Lenten fast. When Moses ascended Mount Sinai to receive the law, "he was there with the Lord forty days and forty nights; he neither ate bread nor drank water" (Ex 34:28), and Elijah, in the same Sinai desert, "arose, and ate and drank, and went in the strength of that food forty days and forty nights to Horeb, the mount of God" (1 Kings 19:8). And from the New Testament, Jesus Christ himself is our model for fasting and prayer during the forty days of Lent, when we purify our heart for Easter so that we might walk illuminated by the light of his resurrection, renewed in body, mind, and spirit. Christ sanctifies us, and our part is to go with him into the desert, to pass the forty days there with him in prayer and fasting, silence and solitude.

SPECIALISTS IN CONTEMPLATION

"And after six days Jesus took with him Peter and James and John, and led them up a high mountain apart by themselves; and he was transfigured before them, and his garments became glistening, intensely white, as no fuller on earth could bleach them" (Mk 9:2-3).

Jesus allows Peter, James, and John a glimpse of his glory in his Transfiguration. The splendor which they saw in Jesus on this high mountain was normally hidden from their eyes, yet it was his true glory shining through the covering of his humanity. Jesus wanted them to have this physical glimpse of his glory to strengthen them in their faith in him.

It is the same with us. We do not always see the splendor of Jesus Christ. We simply live a life of faith and faithfulness in our following of him, trying always to do his will. But from time to time, he manifests himself to us in his glory, and we experience him shining in our heart, illuminating us from within. Some people only rarely experience this, while others live often in his splendor, illumined by him.

For the sake of this experience, Jesus led these three disciples "up a high mountain apart by themselves" (Mk 9:2). It was not in the midst of the crowd that they had this vision. It was on top of a high mountain where they went to pray (Lk 9:28). They were by themselves, apart, alone.

Times like these are essential for a disciple of Jesus Christ. We need to go apart, by ourselves, alone often, as Jesus did to be alone with his Father in prayer on a mountain at night or in the desert very early in the morning before dawn. As a man, he needed this time alone with God. And we need it also. We have to persevere in this even when we do not experience anything special and when we only want to sleep. By regularly doing this, Christ may frequently reveal himself to us in his glory in our heart.

For the sake of these heavenly manifestations, we should also try to keep our mind free from unnecessary distractions. We should not read everything. We should have custody of our *mind* as well as of our eyes, and not only concerning sexual matters. This is why strict monks, like Carthusians, do not read newspapers or watch television or movies or listen to the radio. We must have custody of our mind, as well as of our eyes, if we want to be contemplatives.

It is also good—if God so calls us—to go apart not only once in a while, but even to live apart, alone, on a high mountain, as specialists whose specialty is contemplation, and to do so for the enrichment of the whole Church. This is how monks try to live. But other Christians too can try to live at least something of this specialty for the spiritual enrichment of us all.

A Vocation Within a Vocation

"Therefore, behold, I will allure her, and bring her into the desert and speak to her heart" (Hosea 2:14).

This is the call to the desert, the time of Israel's espousal to the Lord, when she had left Egypt but before she knew the idols of Canaan. It was a time of purity of heart, of espousal, of the first fruits of her love for the Lord.

The desert became a symbol of Israel's ideal of living only for the Lord, without other distractions. "It was I who knew you in the wilderness, in the land of drought," says the Lord (Hos 13:5). The desert does not have other pleasures, which divide the heart, or other interests or attractions. Only God exists in the desert.

So did the prophets remember their time in the desert. "I remember the devotion of your youth," says the Lord, "your love as a bride, how you followed me in the desert, in a land not sown. Israel was holy to the Lord, the first fruits of his harvest" (Jer 2:2–3). The prophets remembered Israel's time in the desert as an ideal time, a lost ideal, which they longed to return to. "I will again make you dwell in tents, as in the days of the appointed feast," says the Lord (Hos 12:9).

The desert is an ideal for us as well. There are the Desert Fathers, desert monasticism, and the eremitic or desert life. It is the ideal of silence and solitude filled with God, a luminous silence that enables us to commune with God, and "With joy ... draw water from the wells of salvation" (Is 12:3). Then, from this encounter with God in the desert, we can enrich the whole Church, raising the spiritual level in general through the holiness of our life, through our witness, prayer, sermons, writings, and other forms of ministry.

This has always been an ideal in the Church from the days of the Desert Fathers; and there will always be those who experience this call and attraction more than others: people like Isaac the Syrian, Seraphim of Sarov, Theophan the Recluse, Charles de Foucauld, and Thomas Merton. There will always be voices in the desert, like John the Baptist, preparing the way of the Lord (Is 40:3).

God calls and directs certain people in this way, because he wants them to live in greater silence and solitude than the majority of believers, and even than the majority in their own religious or monastic communities. Always, in every religious community, there will be those whom God is calling to this kind of a life of more silence and solitude than the rest. It is an interior call, which one should follow and faithfully obey if God is calling one in that way. Then, through his example, prayer, sermons, and writings, he can enrich his whole community, order, Church, and the world in general.

In this solitude, one has a greater opportunity to read and reflect on the lives and writings of the saints, and thus come to a deeper appreciation of the new life that we have in Jesus Christ in being born again through faith in him. The solitary deeply contemplates the atonement and the new life that flows from the cross and resurrection of Jesus Christ; and he lives without the diversions and entertainments of this world.

He lives a life of continual fasting, renouncing fancy, worldly dishes, delicacies, and the delights of the table, eating but the plain, simple fare of the desert. He lives in great simplicity, focusing only on God with all his heart, far from the distractions, temptations, attractions, and diversions of this world. He seeks to have a heart that is undivided in its love of God. And through his writings, he seeks to share with his community, his order, and the world in general the riches of his experience in Christ.

The Church should always respect and safeguard this precious—although rare—vocation of desert life, the solitary life, and should not consider it an aberration. It is a holy calling of God, a special vocation, a vocation within a vocation, given to but a few, yet meant for the enrichment of all. "Behold, I will allure her and bring her into the desert" (Hos 2:14).

THE WAY OF THE FEW

"Teacher, which is the great commandment in the law? And he said to him, You shall love the Lord your God with all your heart, and with all your soul, and with all your mind. This is the great and first commandment" (Mt 22:36–38).

This is the first commandment of Jesus Christ. It is the most important thing in the world for a Christian. After being saved by our faith in Christ, we should concentrate on this first commandment.

The first commandment is connected with the ideal of evangelical poverty. By practicing evangelical poverty we love God with all our heart, soul, and mind—that is, with all our resources, with our whole being. This is why the poor are the ones Jesus pronounces blessed (Lk 6:20), especially the poor in spirit (Mt 5:3). It is because they live only for God. They are the *anawim*, the poor of the Lord, who are truly happy and blessed. They are blessed because their heart has been purified of other things, of idols, of other gods, of foreign and false gods, and they now live only for the Lord with all their heart, poor in this world. They live for God in simplicity and plainness, a simple, basic life without adornment.

This first commandment is also related to fasting. The rich man who "feasted sumptuously every day" (Lk 16:19) has already divided his heart and already had his reward in this present life. Better by far is a life of prayer and fasting in the desert, far from the world with its delights and pleasures. The monastic life is such a life in the desert, lived only for God, a life of sacrifice and of the renunciation of the world for the sake of the delights of the spirit and of the new creation. This is why monks fast and live in the desert. It is because they want to purify their heart and focus themselves only on God. They want to fulfill the first commandment and love God with all their strength, without division of heart. They do not want to hear from Abraham what the rich glutton Dives heard when he arrived in hell after having "feasted sumptuously every day" (Lk 16:19). Abraham said to him, "Son, remember that you in your *lifetime received your* good things" (Lk 16:25). We need to pay attention to Jesus' words when he said, "woe to you that are rich, for you *have received* your consolation (Lk 6:24).

If we pay heed to the first commandment and live it well, we will be able to avoid the condemnation of those who have *already had* their reward in the good things of this present life. To love the Lord with all our heart, soul, and mind, means not to divide our heart among the pleasures of this world, but rather to live as the blessed poor in spirit. Hence many have chosen to live a life of prayer and fasting in the desert, far from the world and its pleasures.

But how many live according to this ideal? Very few, even among religious, for this is the narrow way of the *few* that leads to life, not the wide and comfortable way of the *many* that leads to destruction (Mt 7:13–14). "Enter by the narrow gate; for the gate is wide and the way is easy, that leads to destruction, and those who enter by it are *many*. For the gate is narrow and the way is hard, that leads to life, and those who find it are *few*" (Mt 7:13-14). May we be among the few who find it.

Part II
The Living Desert:
The Ascetical Dimension of
Desert Living

Do You Want to Find or Lose Your Life?

"He who finds his life will lose it, and he who loses his life for my sake will find it" (Mt 10:39).

A whole philosophy of life is contained in this verse. It is a new way of living in this world, and it is the exact opposite of the philosophy of the world, which tells us that we should save our life in this world in a worldly way, filling our life with its pleasures. In the face of this worldly philosophy, Jesus presents his doctrine of the cross. According to Jesus' new doctrine, those who live according to this worldly philosophy will die and lose their life in vain: "He who finds his life will lose it" (Mt 10:39). Only those who lose their lives in this world for the sake of Jesus Christ will truly find and save their life.

This is the teaching of the few, because the majority will always choose the philosophy and the so-called wisdom of this world, which tells us that to be happy we have to find our life and our happiness here below in this world, in its delights, delicacies, and pleasures. But Jesus teaches us that if we live in this worldly way, we will not be able to keep the first and most important commandment of all, which is to love God with *all* our heart, mind, soul, and strength (Mk 12:30). One who is every day seeking his delight here below has already divided his heart and can no longer love God with *all* his heart. He has not reserved his heart for God alone but is rather dissipating it amid the unnecessary pleasures of this life.

Only he who loses his life in this world for the love of Christ can fulfill the first and most important commandment. Only he who loses his life in this world can love God as he should, with *all* his heart and life. Only he who loses his life in this world can purify his senses and his spirit from other things, appetites, and pleasures, to live for God alone and find his happiness only in him. Only he who loses his life in this world will be purified in his five senses and in the three faculties of his spirit (mind, memory, and will) to enter into union with God in contemplative prayer.

This is the authentic way of life, the hard and narrow way, which few know and even fewer choose, but it is the only way of life (Mt 7:13–14). The majority will always choose the wide and easy way that leads to destruction, the way of the wisdom of this world, the way of finding and saving one's life in a worldly way in the delights of the table and here below in general.

You have to decide which way you want: the *difficult* way of life, of the few; or the *easy* way of destruction, of the many. Do you want to find or lose your life? The choice is yours.

These are the principles. The real adventure begins when we actually put ourselves out on a limb and begin to live by them. Some will go off and live alone in solitude because they want to live in unbroken silence with the Lord through the whole course of their day and not have to socialize with others at meals, for example. This is the eremitic life taken in its more literal sense. It leads to a whole new adventure of the spirit. Others radically reconstruct their diet to avoid all unnecessary pleasures. Others guard themselves from reading newspapers or listening to the radio or watching television or movies and so purify their minds of stimuli and images for the sake of a pure heart for contemplative prayer. All these principles lead to many different adventures of the spirit. May we be among the few who take this path less traveled.

You Cannot Serve
Two Masters

"No one can serve two masters; for either he will hate the one and love the other, or he will be devoted to the one and despise the other. You cannot serve God and mammon" (Mt 6:24).

This verse is the key to understanding the Christian life—that is, the life of the regenerate, of those who have been born again in Jesus Christ through faith. The Holy Spirit makes them a new creature with new interests, with a new orientation, and with a new ethic. They now live by the ethic of the Kingdom of God. All of this means that they now live only for God in every aspect of their life. They no longer live for the delights of food and drink, nor are they any more concerned about the beauty of their clothing. They seek only the Kingdom of God and his justice. They want to be justified by God, made new and resplendent by him, forgiven for their sins and imperfections, and at peace with him. So Jesus says, "seek ye first the kingdom of God, and his righteousness; and all these things shall be added unto you" (Mt 6:33 KJV).

"Therefore I tell you," Jesus says, "do not be anxious about your life, what you shall eat or what you shall drink, nor about your body, what you shall put on" (Mt 6:25). Our concentration should not be divided like this, but rather focused only on God, on one Master only, not on two masters, not on many masters. You cannot serve two masters well. You cannot serve both God and mammon well at the same time. Mammon is the delicacies and delights of this world, the pleasures of the world, which divide the heart. Jesus teaches us that we cannot love or be well devoted both to God and to mammon. We are, rather, to eat simple, basic, ordinary, and healthy foods, and not involve ourselves with worldly clothing or the delights of this world in the matter of food, drink, and clothing—the basic elements human of life. Then we will be able to put all our concentration only on God, as did the poor of the Lord, the poor in spirit, the *anawim* of Yahweh.

It will be very difficult, on the other hand, for a rich man, who is concerned about all these things—about mammon—to enter into the Kingdom of God (Mt 19:24). It would be like a camel trying to get through the eye of a needle (Mt 19:24), for he has *already had* his reward in the delights of this present life (Lk 6:24; 16:25). "…the kingdom of God," says St. Paul, "does not mean food and drink but righteousness and peace and joy in the Holy Spirit" (Rom 14:17).

Each one will be inspired with his own way of living uniquely for the Lord. There are the forest dwellers, the hermits, who live alone in the mountains, amid nature, and sacrifice conversation with others to be in continual silence, solitude, and dialogue with the Lord in their hearts. This eremitic life may take many forms, but it is an inspiration, an ideal, that moves many to pattern their lives in the direction of greater solitude and silence.

The first commandment of Jesus is, therefore, to "love the Lord your God with all your heart, and with all your soul, and with all your mind, and with all your strength" (Mk 12:30). If we were to do this, we would not divide our heart with mammon and with the pleasures of this world, but would rather love God as our only Master and only treasure (Mt 6:19–21). This is important, "For where your treasure is, there will your heart be also" (Mt 6:21).

OUR CELIBATE LOVE OF THE LORD

"I want you to be free from care. The unmarried man cares about the things of the Lord, how to please the Lord; but the married man cares about the things of the world, how to please his wife, and he is divided. And the unmarried woman or virgin cares about the things of the Lord, how to be holy in body and spirit; but the married woman cares about the things of the world, how to please her husband" (1 Cor 7:32–34).

The consecrated life is the religious life, the life that has renounced the world to live for God alone with all the love of our heart, without any division whatsoever, not even the division of having a human spouse in Christian matrimony. Religious are therefore celibate, that is, married to Christ (2 Cor 11:2) in a way that is so exclusive that it even excludes a human spouse, so that all the love of their heart goes only to the Lord, and is not divided among other things, interests, or persons of this world, not even with a human spouse in the sacrament of matrimony. Priests also, in the Western Church, live this mystery of celibacy. The religious and consecrated life, together with the celibate priesthood, has suffered much in our times in certain countries, and there has been a drastic fall off in vocations to this form of life in these same countries over the past forty years.

How beautiful is this form of life, in which all our time is dedicated to God alone and is free from cares about a wife and children and maintaining a home and supporting and educating a family! In such a life, we live in solitude and silence with God, focused on our work. We are concerned about our ministry, which God has given us, a ministry that we exercise out of love for God, preaching the Gospel and ministering to the needs of others.

A religious normally lives in community with other consecrated persons who confirm and support him in his vocation and dedication; or he lives a solitary life, alone with God in silence, prayer, and fasting, renouncing the pleasures of this life. He does this in order to live a holy life without division of heart in his love and service of God. The consecrated, religious, and celibate life is in many ways, as St. Paul says, a life "free from care" (1 Cor 7:32), a life supremely concentrated and focused on the Lord in love and dedication. All our psychic, physical, affective, and spiritual energies are focused and concentrated on the Lord, and on his ministry.

The consecrated life is, moreover, lived in personal solitude, even if one lives in community, and in this solitude one finds the best opportunity for silent contemplative prayer, daily meditation on the scriptures, and time without interruption or distraction for spiritual reading of good books, which edify and nourish the spirit.

Hence St. Paul says, "I want you to be free from care" (1 Cor 7:32). And he goes on to say, "The unmarried man cares about the things of the Lord, how to please the Lord" (1 Cor 7:32). He is free from care about the world in general, and free from concern about a wife and family. And so, as St. Paul says, he is not *divided*. On the other hand, "the married man cares about the things of the world, how to please his wife, and he *is divided*" (1 Cor 7:33–34). St. Paul wants to free us from this division, so that our hearts may be without any division whatsoever if we are called to the consecrated, religious, or celibate life.

We see in the Bible that the life of a widow, if one lives it faithfully, is a form of religious life. In other words, a true widow lives a solitary life, dedicated to God alone in every aspect of her life. St. Paul says, "She who is a real widow, and is left all alone, has set her hope on God and continues in supplications and prayers night and day; whereas she who lives in pleasures is dead even while she lives" (1 Tim 5:5–6). The true widow, according to St. Paul, lives for God alone, renouncing the pleasures of this world. She is like the widowed prophetess Ana, who was present at the Presentation of Jesus, and who "did not depart from the temple, worshiping with fasting and prayer night and day" (Lk 2:37). Judith is another true widow. "Judith had lived at home as a widow for three years and four months" and she "girded sackcloth about her loins and wore the garments of her widowhood. She fasted all the days of her widowhood" (Judith 8:4–6).

We see then that the life of a true widow, like that of a true religious, consecrated person, or celibate, is a life of prayer, fasting, and the renunciation of the pleasures of life in order to have a truly undivided heart in her devotion and dedication to the Lord alone—a life and a heart not divided by other pleasures. It is for this reason that the Church has always taught—and still teaches (see the Appendix)—that the consecrated, religious, and celibate life for the Kingdom of God is superior to matrimony. It is because it enables us to live with greater facility with an undivided heart in our love of God.

A life alone with God is a great ideal. It leads many into the adventure of solitude, into the forest, into the wilderness, into the mountains, into the desert, to be in communion with the Lord in the heart, without distraction. This ideal is at the heart of the eremitic life, the more solitary branch of religious life. We only need the courage to begin to put such an ideal into practice for our life to be changed and enriched. May many be encouraged by the beauty of this ideal to make their own experiments with it.

WHY CELIBACY?

"For there are eunuchs who have been so from birth, and there are eunuchs who have been made eunuchs by men, and there are eunuchs who have made themselves eunuchs for the sake of the kingdom of heaven. He who is able to receive this, let him receive it" (Mt 19:12).

This is an important Biblical text for celibacy. Jesus says here that there are those who do not marry for the sake of the Kingdom of God, that is, they have made themselves eunuchs in a figurative sense by not marrying. So we see that the Kingdom of God can be a legitimate and good motive for renouncing marriage. One renounces marriage and family in order to dedicate himself more exclusively to God and to the Kingdom of God, to a life of prayer, solitude, renunciation of the world, silence, sacrifice, fasting, and ministry. One can do all these important things *better* if he does not have a wife and family. Jesus, therefore, blesses more the one who "has left house or wife or brothers or parents or children, for the sake of the kingdom of God." He will "receive manifold more in this time, and in the age to come eternal life" (Lk 18:29–30).

The celibate can better serve only one Master (Mt 6:24). His heart can remain integral in its love for God, without the division of a human love. He can better renounce the pleasures of this world, and live only for God with all his heart, all his soul, all his mind, and all his strength (Mk 12:30). And this is the most important thing. It is the first commandment.

St. Paul therefore writes, "It is well for a man not to touch a woman" (1 Cor 7:1), and "I wish that all were as I myself am," that is, celibate (1 Cor 7:7). He also said, "To the unmarried and the widows I say that it is well for them to remain single as I do" (1 Cor 7:8). And about virgins he says, "So he who marries his virgin does well; and he who refrains from marriage will do better" (1 Cor 7:38). Concerning widows, he says that they are free to marry again, "But in my judgment she is happier if she remains as she is" (1 Cor 7:39–40).

Finally, St. Paul says, "The unmarried man is anxious about the affairs of the Lord, how to please the Lord; but the married man is anxious about worldly affairs, how to please his wife, and he is divided" (1 Cor 7:32–34). Celibacy better enables us to live only for the Lord, without being divided. The celibate has a life of greater silence and solitude for God, and for spiritual reading and prayer. Without a family, he can remain in much silence, and live a simpler and more austere life, only for God, more separated from the world, from television, movies, secular music, and other invasions of the world, which distract and divide the heart. As a result, the celibate, dedicated in this way more exclusively to God and to his Kingdom, can also better exercise the ministry of preaching the word of salvation in Jesus Christ.

PREPARING IN THE DESERT THE WAY OF THE LORD

"Behold, I send my messenger before thy face, who shall prepare thy way; the voice of one crying in the wilderness: Prepare the way of the Lord, make his paths straight … Now John was clothed with camel's hair, and had a leather girdle around his waist, and ate locusts and wild honey" (Mk 1:2–3,6).

John the Baptist is our model in many ways. He was sent by God to prepare his way in the desert and to make straight his paths. He did this by clothing himself with camel's hair, wearing a leather girdle around his waist, and eating locusts and wild honey in the desert (Mk 1:6). He did this because, like the prophets who dressed this way before him (Zech 13:4; 2 Kings 1:8), he wanted to live for God alone in a radical and visible way. He lived like this because he wanted to love God with all his heart, with all his soul, and with all his strength (Dt 6:5). He did not want to divide his heart among the delights of this world. He also did this because he sought a life of silence and solitude with God, without distraction. So he lived, says St. Luke, in the desert from his youth up, and wore the clothing and ate the food of the desert. "…the child grew," says St. Luke, "and became strong in spirit, and he was in the desert till the day of his manifestation to Israel" (Lk 1:80).

Having lived intimately with God in this way, in his cave in the desert, when the word of God came to him in the desert (Lk 3:2), he was ready, and he began his career of being "the voice of one crying in the desert: Prepare the way of the Lord, make straight his paths" (Mk 1:3). His life in the desert prepared him for his mission to call Israel to repentance in preparation for the coming of God into the world.

Now is the time in which we also prepare the way of the Lord and make his paths straight. And we do it as John did it, in the desert, living only for God with all our heart, all our soul, and all our strength. We need to spend time with John in a cave in the desert, eating locusts and wild honey and clothing ourselves with camel's hair and with a leather girdle around our waist (Mk 1:6).

And what is it that we are doing in the desert with John? We are preparing the way of the Lord, that his Kingdom might come, that the world might be transformed into the Kingdom of God.

It is Jesus Christ, through our faith in him, who makes us resplendent before God with his righteousness (Is 61:10). It is his death on the cross that has won for us the forgiveness of our sins and has removed from us the burden of our guilt when we invoke him with faith, especially in the sacrament of reconciliation.

Christ then wants us to cooperate with this great gift and bear good fruit in a virtuous life. It is to do this that we go into the desert with John. It is so that the gift of Christ might extend itself to every aspect of our life. It is not easy to live for God with all our heart in this world, for there are so many distractions, pleasures, delights, and temptations that attract our heart away from him in every direction. This is why monks have always fled from the world and gone to the desert, so that they could live for God alone, as did John the Baptist, with all their heart.

This is the contemplative life, the desert life. This is the best context for contemplation, for union with God in light during prayer and all the day long. Our whole life has to be contemplative, not only our times of prayer. We have to empty ourselves of other things for the sake of God in every aspect of our life, and John the Baptist is our model, preparing the way of the Lord. God comes to us more richly in the desert, when we eat more simply, dress more simply, and live in greater silence and solitude, far from the pleasures and distractions of the world—in the wilderness, in a wasteland, in the desert, like John the Baptist. By doing this, we discover that the desert is the place *par excellence* for experiencing God's interior light and heavenly peace; and we discover for ourselves that monks were not mistaken in their predilection for the desert for living in intimacy with God.

Let us, therefore, prepare in the desert the way of the Lord. Where is your desert? How do you live in the desert with John the Baptist?

The Humble Rejoice in the Lord

"The meek shall obtain fresh joy in the Lord, and the poor among men shall exult in the Holy One of Israel" (Is 29:19).

Isaiah is prophesying the Messianic age as a time of joy. In those days, he says, "the poor among men shall exult in the Holy One of Israel" (Is 29:10). Those who will experience this joy are the humble of the earth, for "The meek shall obtain fresh joy in the Lord" (Is 29:19). The poorest and humblest are the ones who will rejoice in the Messianic times. It is the poorest of the poor, who have no other source from which they can find happiness, who will rejoice in the Lord in the Messianic days. The humble and meek are those who have nothing in this world. They have lost everything and remain with the Lord alone as their only source of joy in life. The world rejects them, not recognizing or accepting them. They remain locked out of its pleasures and honors, and do not follow its values. But it is they, the humble and the poor among men, not the rich of this world, who will rejoice in the Lord in the days of the Messiah.

We are now in that Messianic age. Jesus Christ is our Messiah and Savior. He gives us great relief and jubilation of spirit through the forgiveness of our sins, and he removes from us the sadness and pain of our guilt. He takes away our guilt. He does this through the merits of his death on the cross for those who believe in those merits and invoke them with faith. Then, in his resurrection, his splendor illuminates us, and we walk in its light, which is a new light in our life and heart. We rise to new life in him.

But who are those who most experience this? They are the humble, the meek, the poorest of the poor, the *anawim* of Yahweh, the poor of the Lord.

And who are the poor of the Lord, the *anawim* today? They are those who have left all else, to remain only with God as their only source of happiness. They are those who follow John the Baptist into the desert, living in a cave, clothing themselves with camel's hair and eating locusts and wild honey (Mk 1:6). If we have other sources of happiness besides the Lord, we will not experience so much happiness in the Lord. And to rejoice always (1 Thess 5:16) in the Lord, we need to love Christ alone; that is, we need to live a humble, poor, and simple life, looking to him alone for our joy. We need to be the humble of the earth, the *anawim* of Yahweh. It is then that we will grow in our joy in the Lord and "exult in the Holy One of Israel" (Is 29:19). We will rejoice in him in the midst of the problems and illnesses of life. And the less we have in this world, the more we will rejoice in the Lord.

Renouncing the World

"…always carrying in the body the death of Jesus, so that the life of Jesus may also be manifested in our bodies" (2 Cor 4:10).

St. Paul speaks about the cross in his life. Christ saved us by his cross, and then he recommended it to us as a way of life if we want to follow him. St. Paul says that he always carries the death of Jesus, thus living himself the mystery of the cross, so that the life of Jesus might also manifest itself in him. Jesus told us, "If anyone would come after me, let him deny himself and take up his cross and follow me" (Mk 8:34). This is the true path of the disciple of Jesus, namely, taking up the cross and following him. We are to renounce all, carry the cross, and follow him. But if we try to save our life in this world by renouncing the cross, we will lose our life with God. If, on the other hand, we accept the way of life of the cross, the life of renouncing the world and all things, we will save our life with God (Mk 8:35).

The cross is our new way of living as Christians. It means renouncing the world to live only for God. We are to sacrifice our life for the love of Christ. This is to live in the Spirit and not according to the flesh. We are to live the life of the new man, directed by the Spirit of God and no longer according to the desires of the flesh, for "To set the mind on the flesh is death, but to set the mind on the Spirit is life and peace" (Rom 8:6). And "whoever would save his life will lose it; and whoever loses his life for my sake and the gospel's will save it" (Mk 8:35). For "He who loves his life loses it, and he who hates his life in this world will keep it for eternal life" (Jn 12:25). These sayings apply to all Christians, to each in accordance with his state in life.

This means that we have to be crucified to the world, and the world to us (Gal 6:14). We die to the world in order to live only for God. If we are occupied with the pleasures of this world, we will not be reserved for the Lord alone. Therefore we glory with St. Paul in the cross. "But far be it from me to glory," he said, "except in the cross of our Lord Jesus Christ, by which the world has been crucified to me, and I to the world" (Gal 6:14).

This is a new way of living in the world, reserving our heart only for God and renouncing all else. This is the sure path, blessed and approved by

Jesus, to obtain the buried treasure and the pearl of great price (Mt 13:44–46). They are obtained only at the price of renouncing all else. As the man who discovered the buried treasure could obtain possession of it only by first selling all that he had in order to be able to buy the field where the treasure was buried, so will we be able to experience the life of Jesus within us only by embracing his cross and renouncing all else for the love of him.

What form will this take for you? Will it lead you to a desert cave, or to a mountain hermitage, to a life of deep silence and profound solitude, to a life in the light, a life with one goal only? What new adventure of the spirit will this call lead you to?

Widows and the *Anawim*, the Poor of the Lord

"And a poor widow came, and put in two copper coins, which make a penny. And he called his disciples to him, and said to them, truly, I say to you, this poor widow has put in more than all those who are contributing to the treasury. For they all contributed out of their abundance; but she out of her poverty has put in everything she had, her whole living" (Mk 12:42–44).

This poor widow who put all that she had into the treasury represents Jesus' ideal, the ideal of evangelical poverty. She is for him one of the *anawim*, the poor of the Lord, who have lost everything of this world, all its pleasures, and remain only with God. They live only for God. This is the ideal of the life of a true widow, who stays inside her house (Judith 8:4), wearing sackcloth and "the garments of her widowhood" (Judith 8:5), "worshiping with fasting and prayer night and day" (Lk 2:37). The true widow "is left all alone, has set her hope on God and continues in supplications and prayers night and day" (1 Tim 5:5). "But she that liveth in *pleasure* is dead while she liveth" (1 Tim 5:6 KJV). The widow Judith "fasted all the days of her widowhood" (Judith 8:6), and the widow Ana, who saw the child Jesus in the temple when she was eighty-four years old, "did not depart from the temple, worshiping with fasting and prayer night and day" (Lk 2:37). Her entire life was dedicated to God in the temple, in prayer and fasting.

St. Paul speaks of widows together with celibates and virgins. He says, "The unmarried man is anxious about the affairs of the Lord, how to please the Lord; but the married man is anxious about worldly affairs, how to please his wife, and he is divided" (1 Cor 7:32–34). To the widows he says, "To the unmarried and the widows I say that it is well for them to remain single as I am" (1 Cor 7:8). And again about the widow he says, "in my judgment she is happier if she remains as she is" (1 Cor 7:40), that is, single.

There are widows today, as in the days of St. Paul, and there are also celibates today, persons living the religious life for the love of God in order to have an undivided heart in their love for God and in their service of him, serving day and night in prayer and fasting. It is this ideal that we need to meditate on, the ideal of the religious life, celibate for the Kingdom of God, the ideal of priestly celibacy, the ideal of the life of a true widow. It is a life of simplicity and austerity that renounces the pleasures of this life and of this creation, for those of the Kingdom of God and of the new creation. It is a life with God, in which we seek our joy only in him, and not in the delights of this present life (Col 3:1–2). It is a life of prayer and fasting, of meditation, spiritual reading, and evangelical poverty. This is the life that has the hundredfold reward (Mt 19:29).

This is a life separated from the world and its attractions and distractions that divide our heart from an undivided love of God alone. That is why it is lived in reclusion, living inside one's house, or not leaving the temple, dressed differently, in widow's dress, marking them off still further from the world. It is spent in fasting and prayer, denying oneself the delights of this world to better live for those of God.

A HEART RESERVED
FOR GOD ALONE

"Which commandment is the first of all? Jesus answered, The first is, Hear, O Israel: The Lord our God, the Lord is one; and you shall love the Lord your God with all your heart, and with all your soul, and with all your mind, and with all your strength" (Mk 12:28–30).

This is the first commandment for all who believe in Jesus Christ. It is not just for some special group within the Church. It is not just for priests and religious. It is not just for celibates who have even renounced Christian marriage in order to love God alone with all the love of their heart, without any division, not even the division of loving a Christian spouse within the sacrament of matrimony. This commandment is rather the first commandment for every Christian.

Christ wants us to love God with all our resources—that is, with all our energy, intelligence, strength, heart, mind, and soul. This is his first and most important commandment. He wants our whole heart, all the love of our heart, all of our work, all of our time, all of our dedication. In whatever state of life we are in, he wants all of us, to the degree that we are able to offer and dedicate ourselves in this way while still fulfilling the obligations and responsibilities of our state in life. This is why the Church has always taught (and still teaches) that celibacy is a higher call than marriage (see the Appendix on this point), namely, because the celibate can love God with less division of heart, that is, with a heart more completely and radically undivided in its love for God, and for him alone, thus fulfilling the most important commandment of all in a still more radical way. But in this way of life, the celibate functions as a mirror for the whole Church, showing it in a clearer and more radical way what everyone should strive to do, each in accord with the responsibilities of his own state in life.

In fact, in the world of the resurrection, everyone will be celibate, for "those who are accounted worthy to attain to that age and to the resurrection from the dead neither marry nor are given in marriage" (Lk 20:35), but "are like the angels in heaven" (Mk 12:25). Everyone will be celibate because only "The sons of this age marry or are given in marriage" (Lk 20:34).

Those who now in this present age are already celibate for the love of God are, therefore, eschatological signs, that is, signs of the future, reminding the whole Church of her own future state, serving as mirrors for her to see her own future in seeing those who are celibate now, ahead of time.

Every Christian is, therefore, called to live by this greatest of all commandments, which is to live in simplicity, following the spirit of evangelical poverty, not dividing his heart among the pleasures, delicacies, and delights of this world. All are called to love God with all their heart, in accordance with the responsibilities of their state in life.

And, as Jesus added a second commandment, we also know that we are to spend our life helping our neighbor with our gifts and talents. We are to dedicate our lives to helping and saving our neighbor.

St. Benedict
Renounces the World

"Lo, we have left everything and followed you. What then shall we have ... every one who has left houses or brothers or sisters or father or mother or children or lands, for my name's sake, will receive a hundredfold, and inherit eternal life" (Mt 19:27,29).

St. Benedict (480–547) is the father of the monks of the West. He retired from the world and lived in a cave, seeking God. Later, many followed him, and he founded the great monastery of Monte Cassino, and wrote a rule for them. He wanted to leave everything and live only for God in a radically literal way, without worldly possessions, and in simplicity, austerity, and poverty. So he left the world, with its diversions and entertainments, with its pleasures and delights, for a simple and austere life of prayer and fasting in the desert, far from the world, with its noise, superficiality, temptations, attractions, and recreations. According to his rule of life, they lived in silence, never ate breakfast, only ate an evening meal six months out of the year, and did not eat meat.

Monastic life is a life of much silence and solitude, separated from the world, in order to live in a recollected way with the Lord in the silence of the heart and walk in the light of Christ (Jn 8:12). It is a life of heavenly peace, the peace of Christ, which comes through faith. In order to live in this light and peace, monks leave all else and thus seek the hundredfold reward promised to those who leave their homes, family, and other possessions for the love of Christ (Mt 19:29) to live for him alone with all the love of their heart. They leave all else for Christ, as the first disciples left all to follow Jesus. When Jesus said to them, "Follow me, and I will make you fishers of men. Immediately they left their nets and followed him" (Mt 4:19–20). And when he called the sons of Zebedee, "Immediately they left the boat and their father, and followed him" (Mt 4:22).

This is what monks do. They seek only God, leave behind the things and pleasures of the world, the delights of the table, and the fashions of the day, and live a life of prayer and fasting in the desert. They do their silent work, recollected in meditation and prayer, illuminated from within by the light of Christ. Thus the grace of Jesus Christ transforms and sanctifies them, making them lights in the world (Phil 2:15), to illuminate the rest (Mt 5:14-16) and show them the way to life and peace.

They leave everything because they do not want their heart to be distracted or divided by worldly possessions and activities. Monks know that it is difficult for a rich man to enter the Kingdom of heaven (Mt 19:23), and that "it is easier for a camel to go through the eye of a needle than for a rich man to enter the kingdom of God" (Mt 19:24). Therefore, to facilitate their entrance into the Kingdom of God, they make themselves poor for the sake of Christ. They lose their life in this world in order to keep it for God, instead of trying to save their life in a worldly way and lose it with God (Mt 16:25). In fact, they hate their life in this world to keep it with God, because "He who loves his life loses it, and he who hates his life in this world will keep it for eternal life" (Jn 12:25).

A monk lives austerely because he knows that the rich, with their pleasures, delights, and banquets have *already received* their reward, and will inherit nothing further, for Jesus said, "woe to you that are rich, for *you have received* your consolation. Woe to you that are full now, for you shall hunger. Woe to you that laugh now, for you shall mourn and weep" (Lk 6:24–25).

The monk wants only God to be his pleasure and happiness, for otherwise his happiness in God is diluted, divided, and drowned out by other pleasures (Mt 6:24). He, therefore, lives a life of continual fasting and prayer, far from the world—in the desert, a place of little outward attraction. The monk remembers the word of Abraham to the rich man "who was clothed in purple and fine linen and who feasted sumptuously every day" (Lk 16:19), saying to him, "Son, remember that you in your lifetime *received* your good things, and Lazarus in like manner evil things; but now he is comforted here, and you are in anguish" (Lk 16:25). The rich man has *already received* his reward, and so there will be nothing further for him to receive. Therefore the monk does not want to have his good things now, here below. His only reward is Christ, with his light and his love. This is his ideal.

The monk knows that in order to obtain the buried treasure, which is the Kingdom of God, he has to sell all that he has (Mt 13:44). Thus he lives in simplicity and austerity, only for God, who transforms and sanctifies him through the merits of Christ, in order that he might be a light in the world (Phil 2:15) and raise the spiritual level in general.

SIGNS OF FAITH

"And my neighbors laughed at me and said, He is no longer afraid that he will be put to death for doing this; he once ran away, and here he is burying the dead again" (Tobit 2:8).

Tobit was a righteous man of the tribe of Naphtali. He was deported to Nineveh and lost everything when Sennacherib, king of Assyria, sought his life for burying the Israelites slain by the king.

Tobit was a man of faith, justified and saved, not by his good works (Rom 3:28; Gal 2:16), but by his faith (Rom 4:3; Gen 15:6), which manifested itself in good works. He lived in great faithfulness to the law of Moses, even to the point of risking his life. He gives various striking examples of his fidelity to the will of God as revealed in the Mosaic law. He says, "All the tribes that joined in apostasy used to sacrifice to the calf Baal, and so did the house of Naphtali my forefather. But I alone went often to Jerusalem for the feasts, as it is ordained for all Israel by an everlasting decree" (Tobit 1:5–6). He alone had the courage of his convictions to do what was right when everyone else went astray, following the crowd. And he was blessed for this. He was often the only one in his whole tribe who remained faithful to the obligations of the people of God.

"Now when I was carried away captive to Nineveh," he tells us, "all my brethren and my relatives ate the food of the Gentiles; but I kept myself from eating it because I remembered God with all my heart" (Tob 1:10–12). Tobit alone remained faithful to the will of God concerning food when his whole family and all his relatives abandoned the Israelite diet according to the law of God and ate like pagans. And when he recovered his wife, son, and house, after losing them for having buried the Israelites slain by the king, he continued burying the dead as an act of charity, and in this he continued putting his life in danger.

Tobit, in his virtuous life, is an example for all of us. He lived a heroically virtuous life, often being the only one in his environment who did the will of God. We also are called to confess Christ before men (Mt 10:32) and not be ashamed of him (Mk 8:38) or of his will, even if we are the only ones in our environment who remain faithful to our obligations.

There are many examples of this kind of virtue today that can inspire us to remain faithful. Priests, for example, who remain faithful to their obligation to pray the liturgy of the hours and to wear clerical dress (Canons 284; 669; 276) are inspiring examples for all of this kind of fidelity. Such faithfulness can help many in the Church today to imitate their example, each according to the obligations of his state in life.

The exterior obligations of our vocation, faithfully observed, should be expressions and visible signs of our interior devotion and love of God. They are signs of faith that inspire many and are much needed in our world today, so forgetful of God. They should be inspiring outer signs of real interior renewal and devotion. We need outer signs and symbols and don't just invent them on our own. They are given to us in the tradition and have deep culturally recognized value and meaning which speak directly to the heart in ways deeper than words. We have lost much ground in this area in recent years. Genuine renewal calls for greater faithfulness in the future in this area.

How to Contemplate
The Glory of Christ

"The glory which thou hast given me I have given to them" (Jn 17:22).

Christ came into the world that we might see and contemplate his glory, which is the glory in which he lives with the Father. Christ gives us access to God and to the experience of the glory of God in our heart. He wants us to contemplate this glory and thus receive from his fullness (Jn 1:16). He wants us to remain in this glory that he has with the Father (Jn 15:9). He wants us, as we contemplate his glory, to be transformed "from glory to glory" into his own image (2 Cor 3:18). This is why he came, because no one living has seen God and can reveal him to us, except Christ (Jn 1:18). For this reason Christ wants us to be with him, namely, to see and contemplate his glory. "Father," he said, "I desire that they also, whom thou hast given me, may be with me where I am, to behold my glory which thou hast given me in thy love for me" (Jn 17:24). He gave us his glory that we might contemplate it. "The glory which thou hast given me," he said, "I have given to them" (Jn 17:22).

In contemplating the glory of Christ, we contemplate the glory of God, the glory of the Father, the glory of the Trinity. Upon ascending into heaven, Christ sent forth from the Father the Holy Spirit to reveal to us the glory of the Trinity, the glory of Christ shining in our hearts (2 Cor 4:6).

By renouncing the world and its pleasures, we can obtain this hidden treasure, this pearl of great price, namely, contemplating the glory of God in the face of Christ (Mt 13:44–46; 2 Cor 4:6). Those who want to contemplate this glory are invited to live contemplatively—that is, to renounce the pleasures of the world and live only for God (Mt 19:21,29). This call is for all, but especially for those who have responded to the call to the priesthood or religious life, which is indeed, in either case, a whole way of life, a celibate life of prayer, simplicity, and evangelical poverty, working in the Lord's vineyard. This call to live contemplatively is also the call to the monastic life, a life of prayer and fasting in the desert, far from the world and its pleasures and distractions, lived in simplicity and evangelical poverty, dedicated to the contemplation of the glory of God shining on the face of Christ (2 Cor 4:6).

Those who wish to respond to this call and live in and contemplate this glory should *live* contemplatively—that is, renounce the pleasures of the world and live in evangelical poverty and simplicity, for living in this way is the *context* in which we can contemplate the glory of God.

SENT TO THE WORLD,
BUT NOT OF THE WORLD

"I have given them thy word; and the world has hated them because they are not of the world, even as I am not of the world" (Jn 17:14).

As Jesus Christ was not of the world, neither are we, his followers, of the world, nor should we love the world or the things that are in the world. "Do not love the world or the things in the world," says St. John. "If any one loves the world, love for the Father is not in him" (1 Jn 2:15). We are not to be worldly, not to be lovers of the pleasures of the world. "Unfaithful creatures!" says St. James. "Do you not know that friendship with the world is enmity with God? Therefore whoever wishes to be a friend of the world makes himself an enemy of God" (James 4:4).

We are not to find and seek our joy here below in the entertainments and diversions of the world. Rather, as Christians, we are to live a new and risen life in Christ. "If then you have been raised with Christ," says St. Paul, "seek the things that are above, where Christ is, seated at the right hand of God. Set your minds on things that are above, not on things that are on earth" (Col 3:1–2).

Christ did not come into the world to fill himself with its delights, but rather to give his life as a ransom for many (Mk 10:45). And so does he wish us also to live, not as lovers of the world and its pleasures, but as persons sent into the world with a mission to the world, that is, to save the world—to save the world from its own worldliness

To love the world in order to *save* the world is something completely different from loving the world in order to seek its pleasures and live a worldly life. "God so loved the world that he gave his only Son, that whoever believes in him should not perish but have eternal life" (Jn 3:16). This is the sense in which we are to love the world, namely, that we have a mission to the world to save it. We should, therefore, give our life in love for the world, for our brethren, that they might be saved in Jesus Christ. Hence, "the Son of Man also came not to be served but to serve, and to give his life as a ransom for many" (Mk 10:45). He did not come to be served by the pleasures of the world, but to serve and to give his life as an expiation for our sins, suffering our punishment in our place, to free us from this punishment and from our sins and guilt and to give us a new and risen life his resurrection.

In this, Christ is our model. Even though we do not bear the sins of others, we are, nonetheless, to give our life for our friends and brethren, so that they may be saved, saved from the world in its worldliness. "By this we know love," says St. John, "that he laid down his life for us; and we ought to lay down our lives for the brethren" (1 Jn 3:16). It is clear that Christ wants us to follow his example of giving his life for the world. He said, "If I then, your Lord and teacher, have washed your feet, you also ought to wash one another's feet. For I have given you an example, that you also should do as I have done to you" (Jn 13:14–15). This is our mission, to give our life in love for our friends and brethren. "Greater love than this no one has," said Jesus, "that one should lay down his life for his friends" (Jn 15:13). So ought we then do!

It is clear, then, what we are to do. We are not of the world, and the world will hate us because we are different, for we do not seek its pleasures, as do the rest. "They are surprised," says St. Peter, "that you do not now join them in the same wild profligacy, and they abuse you" (1 Peter 4:4). Yes, we are different from the world. The word of God has made us different. "I have given them thy word," said Jesus, "and the world has hated them because they are not of the world, even as I am not of the world" (Jn 17:14). We are not of the world because we do not seek the things of the world, but rather those that are above, "where Christ is, seated at the right hand of God" (Col 3:1). God is our only pleasure, to the degree that this is possible, and so we renounce the unnecessary pleasures of the world. "If you were of the world," said Jesus, "the world would love its own; but because you are not of the world, but I chose you out of the world, therefore the world hates you" (Jn 15:19).

We do not love the world in the sense of a quest for its pleasures (1 Jn 2:15). But yes, we do love the world in the sense that we have a mission to the world to save the world (Jn 3:16). In this second sense, we should imitate the good shepherd, who laid down his life for his sheep (Jn 10:11,15,17). We should, therefore, lay down our life for our brethren, to bring them the word of salvation, to preach Christ to them, for "No one who denies the Son has the Father. [And] He who confesses the Son has the Father also" (1 Jn 2:23), and, "He who has the Son has life; [but] he who has not the Son of God has not life" (1 Jn 5:12). To bring Christ to the world for its salvation is our mission.

We should give the example of the testimony of our life that we are not of the world in the sense of seeking its pleasures (1 Jn 2:15), but rather are persons who have been sent to the world on a mission save the world (Jn 3:16), for "As thou didst send me into the world," Jesus tells us, "so I have sent them into the world" (Jn 17:18).

THE ASCENDED LIFE

"So then the Lord Jesus, after he had spoken to them, was taken up into heaven, and sat down at the right hand of God" (Mk 16:19).

Jesus ascended into heaven, returning to his Father, while we are sent out by him to "preach the gospel to every creature" (Mk 16:15); yet at the same time, we also ascend with him into heaven in spirit. We have risen with him and should therefore now "seek the things that are above, where Christ is, seated at the right hand of God," and set our "minds on things that are above, not on things that are on earth" (Col 3:1–2). This is the risen life, which we should now be living in Jesus Christ. In addition, we also ascend into heaven with him in spirit, and should, therefore, live not only a risen, but even an ascended life in him; for God has "raised us up with him, and made us sit with him in the heavenly places in Christ Jesus" (Eph 2:6).

This should now be the ideal of our new life in Jesus Christ—to live a risen and ascended life in him. We are one with Christ, and so where he is, we also are. Seeking the things that are above and not those of the world means not dividing our heart among worldly delights and pleasures, but rather renouncing them to obtain the buried treasure and pearl of great price (Mt 13:44–46). The man could only obtain the buried treasure by selling everything else first. This teaches us that we can only obtain the treasure of the new life in Christ, risen and ascended with him, by first renouncing all the unnecessary pleasures of this world. In this way, we will respond positively to the call to perfection given to the rich young man (Mt 19:21). This is to seek only the things that are above. If we do this, we are a true disciple, for "whoever of you does not renounce all that he has cannot be my disciple" (Lk 14:33). But if we do this, we will receive the hundredfold reward (Mt 19:29) and will consider all else that we have left "as loss for the sake of Christ" (Phil 3:7).

This, then, is our ideal of the new and ascended life. But at the same time, we will also preach the Gospel to every creature (Mk 16:15) for their salvation through the blood of Christ, knowing that "He who believes and is baptized will be saved; but he who does not believe will be condemned" (Mk

16:16), for "He who believes in him is not condemned, [but] he who does not believe is condemned already" (Jn 3:18).

This is the new life that Christ has given us as he ascends to the Father. In his ascension, "he entered once for all into the Holy Place, taking ... his own blood" (Heb 9:12), thus bringing his sacrifice to its completion and obtaining its results. There, in the heavenly sanctuary, he intercedes for us before his Father (Rom 8:34; Heb 7:25; 9:24), showing him his wounds and blood, with which he absorbed into himself the divine wrath against our sins.

It is this sacrifice that enables us to live a new, forgiven, risen, and ascended life in Christ. According to the eternal plan of God, this sacrifice reconciled God to us, enabling him to *justly* forgive us if we believe in his Son. It is this sacrifice that gives us our ascended life and at the same time sends us out to preach salvation in Christ to every creature (Mk 16:15), being his "witnesses in Jerusalem and in all Judea and Samaria and to the end of the earth" (Acts 1:8).

PERSECUTED BECAUSE NOT OF THIS WORLD

"If you were of the world, the world would love its own; but because you are not of the world, but I chose you out of the world, therefore the world hates you" (Jn 15:19).

We are not of the world if we are Christians. This is clear from the scriptures (Jn 15:19; 17:14,16). The world will, therefore, persecute us because our values are different. The world hates us because we are not of the world. Jesus was not of the world, and neither are we, his followers, of the world. "They are not of the world," Jesus says, "even as I am not of the world" (Jn 17:16). Jesus is not of the world, and, moreover, testifies of it "that its works are evil" (Jn 7:7). Therefore, the world hates him (Jn 7:7). The Christian will be hated, rejected, and persecuted by the world, just as Christ was. This is our vocation and life as his followers. "A servant is not greater than his master," Jesus says. "If they persecuted me, they will persecute you" (Jn 15:20).

They persecuted Jesus because he testified concerning the world "that its works are evil" (Jn 7:7). By the testimony of our life—that is, by our way of living, by our words, by our writings, and by our sermons—we also testify that the works of the world are evil. We testify that worldly entertainments are not worthy of a Christian, and we therefore live in a completely different way. Our whole way of living is completely different from that of the world around us, and so the world hates us and does not accept us. If we were of the world, it would be different. We would be popular and loved by the world.

Unfortunately, however, there are Christians who are ashamed of being Christians and who imitate the world and live like the world. They try, in this way, to avoid being persecuted by the world. Christ will also finally be ashamed of them when he comes in his glory (Mk 8:38).

But blessed are we when we do not imitate the world and when we are hated and persecuted for Christ's sake (Lk 6:22). This should not shake us, even if we see everyone hating us for Christ's sake, for Jesus predicted that this would happen to us as his followers. "…you will be hated by all for my name's sake," he said. "But he who endures to the end will be saved" (Mt 10:22).

We are not of the world, and our whole way of life should testify that a worldly style of life is evil. We should not live in a worldly way; rather we should reject such a way and testify against it. It is our glory and our vocation to live in this different way, as witnesses of Jesus Christ in the world, shining "as lights in the world," "in the midst of a crooked and perverse generation" (Phil 2:15). Let us always remember, then, that we are not of the world, as Christ was not of the world (Jn 17:16). God is our only joy; and this certainly is not true of the world and of its way of living.

THE RICH HAVE ALREADY
RECEIVED THEIR REWARD

"But Abraham said, Son, remember that you in your lifetime received your good things, and Lazarus in like manner evil things; but now he is comforted here, and you are in anguish" (Lk 16:25).

These are the words that Dives, the rich glutton, heard in hell, where he went after his death. During his lifetime, he "was clothed in purple and fine linen and ... feasted sumptuously every day" (Lk 16:19). Now in hell, Abraham explains to him *why* he is there. It is because he lived a life of luxury and pleasure, and "feasted sumptuously every day" (Lk 16:19). He should remember that he *has already received* his good things and his consolation in his lifetime, so that now, after death, there is no more consolation for him, but only the flames of hell. "...remember," said Abraham to him, "that you in your lifetime received your good things" (Lk 6:25). The poor Lazarus, on the other hand, lived in poverty during his lifetime, but now, after death, he is consoled.

Blessed indeed are the poor (Lk 6:20), for they will receive their consolation in a spiritual way now, and after their death, in heaven. But "Woe to you that are rich," says Jesus, "for you *have received* your consolation" (Lk 6:24) in a worldly way in the good things of this life. Jesus also said that "it will be hard for a rich man to enter the kingdom of heaven" (Mt 19:23) for he has already had his consolation in the worldly pleasures of this life—particularly those who "feasted sumptuously every day" (Lk 16:19). And Jesus adds that "it is easier for a camel to go through the eye of a needle than for a rich man to enter the kingdom of God" (Mt 19:24).

How important it then is to separate ourselves from a luxurious life now while we still have the time and not seek our pleasures in a worldly way in this present life. Rather, we are to focus on God and living the mysteries of the cross and resurrection of Jesus Christ, doing his will. We will find our joy in the desert, in contemplative prayer, in a pure conscience, and in the Holy Spirit, as we work in the Lord's vineyard. How different this is from the luxurious life of the rich!

It is difficult for a rich man to enter the Kingdom of God because he is surrounded by pleasures and delights, and if he is indulgent, he will divide his heart among them, and not love God with all his heart. He will rather have idols, which he puts in his heart and serves in place of God. St. James says to the rich, "Come now, you rich, weep and howl for the miseries that are coming upon you … You have lived on the earth in pleasure and luxury; you have fattened your hearts as in a day of slaughter" (James 5:1,5 NKJV).

And you, how do you live? Do you live in the unnecessary delights of the table, like Dives, the rich glutton, feasting "sumptuously every day" (Lk 16:19)? Are you *dividing* your heart between God and the unnecessary delights of the table? Are you living for the flesh? Do you have your consolation in the material things and honors of this life? Or are you living the life of the *anawim*, the poor of the Lord, who live only for God, who have lost all else of this world and live now for him alone, finding their only joy in life in him, but finding it richly? This is the way of the true contemplative, the way of the hermit, the way of the eremitic life, a life that seeks to leave all else and live in solitude with God and find its joy and light in him.

A LIFE ALL OF ONE PIECE

"…if you pour yourself out for the hungry and satisfy the desire of the afflicted, then shall your light rise in the darkness and your gloom be as the noonday" (Is 58:10).

Isaiah teaches us that if we want our fasting to be acceptable before God, and if we want God's blessing on our fast—namely, that "your light shall rise in the darkness and your gloom be as the noonday" (Is 58:10)—then our life must be *all of one piece*. It must not be divided: fasting on the one hand, but then grieving God's Spirit on the other hand in many other ways by not obeying his will in these other things. If our life is divided like this, our fasting will not be acceptable, and God will not bless us.

What, then, do we have to do to please God with our fasting, so that he will bless us? We must pour ourselves "out for the hungry and satisfy the desire of the afflicted" (Is 58:10). We can do this in many ways: by giving alms, by cultivating vegetables and giving them away to food banks, by preaching the Gospel, by writing sermons and publishing them on the internet, etc. In this way, we give both material and spiritual bread to the hungry and to those in need. We also give bread to the poor by showing them love and by speaking kindly and lovingly to them.

But if we want our life to be all of one piece and not divided or self-contradictory, we must also eliminate our faults. We should not waste time uselessly, but rather always be doing something useful for God. We should always be praying or reading something good for our spirit that will build us up in faith, or studying something that will help us to preach better. We could be writing something that will build up the faith of our neighbor or doing something that will help our neighbor, using the gifts God has given us for this purpose. We are not to waste the time God has given us, spending our days and nights in amusements, games, pastimes, and empty diversions.

We are to live our life in an integral way, so that it is all of one piece, not divided, dispersed, and self-contradictory. Thus will our fasting be acceptable, for it will be of one piece with the rest of our life, a life of loving God with all our heart.

"Then shall your light break forth like the dawn," says the Lord (Is 58:8), "then shall your light rise in the darkness and your gloom be as the noonday ... then you shall take delight in the Lord, and I will make you ride upon the heights of the earth" (Is 58:10,14). When your fasting is accompanied by other good works and a good life in the Lord, then will you be blessed in his sight. When your life is all moving in the same direction, then will you be blessed.

GLORYING IN THE CROSS

"And he called to him the *multitude* with his disciples, and said to them, If anyone would come after me, let him deny himself and take up his cross and follow me" (Mk 8:34).

First of all, we notice that this difficult teaching is for *all*; not just for a special group. Jesus preached it to "the *multitude*" (Mk 8:34). He is telling us what we must do to be his followers. The first thing he says is that we are to deny ourselves. This is the same Greek word that is used when Jesus tells Peter that he will deny him three times (Mk 14:30). It is a strong expression, and here it means to disregard our natural desires so that we can take up our cross and sacrifice ourselves for the love of Christ. We are to make our life a sacrifice of praise to God, a hymn of praise, poured out in love and self-gift, in union with Christ's own sacrifice of himself in love to his Father. We are to do what Christ did, and to do it with him.

You are to lose your life in this world for Christ and the Gospel. If you do, you will save your life; but if you do not, you will lose your life with God (Mk 8:35). You are to live a sacrificial life in this world, not a life of luxury. Your life should rather be an offering poured out in love to God.

You are to live only for God, not for yourself. In this, you are to follow the example of Christ's life and death, for "he died for all, that those who live might live no longer for themselves but for him who for their sake died and was raised" (2 Cor 5:15). We are so struck by the fact that the Son of God gave up his life for us, and are so renewed by this gift, that we give up our lives for him and live henceforth no longer for ourselves but for him who died for us. So we deny ourselves, for "None of us lives to himself, and none of us dies to himself. If we live, we live to the Lord, and if we die, we die to the Lord" (Rom 14:7–8).

In this way we lose our life for him (Mk 8:35), we hate our life in this world for love of him (Jn 12:25). We deny ourselves, take up our cross, and follow him (Mk 8:34). The cross both saves us and teaches us how to live. It is the mystery we are to live. We are to pour out our life in love for God. We are to live a life of sacrifice out of love for God. We do so by living in accordance with his will, without being ashamed of it (Mk 8:38), for his will, will cause us to suffer in this world. It will direct us to live for God alone and deny ourselves for the love of him, pouring ourselves out in sacrifice, as a hymn of praise to God.

THE MONASTIC LIFE,
THE IDEAL OF ST. BENEDICT

"Then Peter said in reply, Lo we have left everything and have followed you. What then shall we have?" (Mt 19:27).

Jesus calls us to leave everything for him and promises us a hundredfold reward. He called Simon and Andrew, saying, "Follow me, and I will make you fishers of men" (Mt 4:19). And "Immediately they left their nets and followed him" (Mt 4:20). In calling James and John, "Immediately they left the boat and their father, and followed him" (Mt 4:21–22). We note that they left even their father—everything. St. Luke tells us that these same apostles, "when they had brought their boats to land, they left everything and followed him" (Lk 5:11). And to "Levi, sitting at the tax office," Jesus said, "Follow me. And he left everything, and rose and followed him" (Lk 5:27–28).

For having left everything for Jesus, he promised them "a hundredfold reward," saying, "every one who has left houses or brothers or sisters or father or mother or children or lands, for my name's sake, will receive a hundredfold, and inherit eternal life" (Mt 19:29). Indeed, by leaving everything for Jesus, they made themselves last in this world, but they will be first with God, while those who are first in this world will be last with God, for "many that are first will be last," says Jesus, "and the last first" (Mt 19:30).

St. Benedict is an example of this for us. He left a world full of sin to live alone with God in the wilderness; and later he left even this small wilderness town to live completely alone as a hermit in a cave for three years, a life of prayer, fasting, and purification. Afterwards, many began to recognize his wisdom and follow him, imitating his desert living. He built monasteries for them and wrote a rule to guide them in their monastic life.

St. Benedict "withdrew from the world of men, knowingly unacquainted with its ways and wisely unlearned in its wisdom" (St. Gregory the Great, *Life of St. Benedict; Breviary*). He knew that to obtain the greatest treasure of all, which is hidden from the rest, he would first have to sell all that he had (Mt 13:44–46) and live henceforth for God alone in every aspect of his life. This

101

is the monastic life, a life lived for God alone by renouncing all else. He could have said with St. Paul that "whatever gain I had, I counted as loss for the sake of Christ" (Phil 3:7). All the pleasures of this world, its delicate food and the luxurious life of the rich, he left behind to obtain this treasure, this divine wisdom, which he bequeathed to his disciples, the monks. All the things that were once gain for him, he now "counted as loss for the sake of Christ. Indeed," he could say with St. Paul, "I count everything as loss because of the surpassing worth of knowing Christ Jesus my Lord. For his sake I have suffered the loss of all things, and count them as refuse, in order that I may gain Christ" (Phil 3:7–8).

St. Benedict had to renounce all these things and leave them behind in order to obtain the greatest treasure of all, just as the "merchant in search of fine pearls" had first to sell all that he had in order to buy the one pearl of great price (Mt 13:45–46).

So St. Benedict renounced his secular clothing and the town where he dwelt to live in the wilderness, in a cave, losing all the things of this world for the sake of Christ, and he counted them as rubbish in comparison with the riches he thereby gained. The opposite of this are those who "live as enemies of the cross of Christ. Their end is destruction, their god is the belly, and they glory in their shame, with minds set on earthly things" (Phil 3:18–19). These are they who seek their pleasures here below in the delights of this world, and know nothing of the riches of Christ and the glory of the cross, "by which the world has been crucified to me, and I to the world," as St. Paul affirms (Gal 6:14). In St. Benedict and in the monastic life, we see the splendor of the cross and the beauty of desert living, namely, a life lived for God alone in every aspect of our life.

Do you feel called to the desert life? If you do, seek for a way to make this dream come true for you. Do not fear to go out on a limb. There is no other way of realizing this dream, and you have but one life in which to try it.

Strangers and Exiles
on Earth

"But recall the former days in which, after you were illuminated, you endured a great struggle with sufferings: partly while you were made a spectacle both by reproaches and tribulations ... and joyfully accepted the plundering of your goods, knowing that you have a better and an enduring possession for yourselves in heaven" (Heb 10:32–34 NKJV).

The author here reminds the Hebrews of their first days after baptism, called here their illumination—that is, when they "were illuminated" (Heb 10:32). In those days, they were happy to be "strangers and exiles on the earth" (Heb 11:13). In those days, he says, they were despoiled of their goods in this world (Heb 10:34), but they accepted it joyfully, hoping for better things in heaven (Heb 10:34). They also suffered reproaches and "were made a spectacle" (Heb 10:34).

This is the condition of a true Christian in every age. For his faith and word of preaching, he will suffer in this world, which will neither understand nor accept him. We are to live as "strangers and exiles on the earth" (Heb 11:13). St. Peter says, "Beloved, I beg you as aliens and exiles, abstain from fleshly lusts which wage war against the soul" (1 Peter 2:11), and, "conduct yourselves with fear throughout the time of your exile," for "You know that you were ransomed from the futile ways inherited from your fathers ... with the precious blood of Christ" (1 Peter 1:17–19).

We are redeemed, washed, and made clean and new by the blood of Christ. We should, therefore, express our gratitude to God for the blood of his Son, poured out in sacrifice on the cross for us to absorb the divine wrath against us for our sins, thus giving us a new and illuminated life in Christ, a life now different from that of the world. Thus the blood of Christ washes us and makes us "strangers and exiles on the earth" (Heb 11:13), renouncing the worldly desires of our former way of life when we lived in the pleasures of this life. And we live now like the *anawim*, the poor of the Lord, who have lost everything and remain only with God.

And so we will become a spectacle to the world, as were the apostles, "For I think," says St. Paul, "that God has exhibited us apostles as last of all, like those sentenced to death; because we have become a spectacle to the world, to angels and to men" (1 Cor 4:9).

Thus, like the poor of Yahweh, we have only God in this world for our happiness, having lost the other pleasures of life. But in this state—washed and cleansed by the blood of Christ—we are happier than all the rest. It is a truly joyful life, washed and cleansed in the blood of Christ, and lived for God alone in the joy of the Holy Spirit. This is the life of a stranger and exile on the earth for the love of God. We make ourselves strangers on earth to be alone with God in love, in solitude, and in silence; and God rewards us accordingly, both in this life and the next.

Preparing the Way
in the Desert

"They said to him then, Who are you? Let us have an answer for those who sent us. What do you say about yourself? He said, I am the voice of one crying in the desert, Make straight the way of the Lord, as the prophet Isaiah said" (Jn 1:22–23).

This is the vocation of John the Baptist, to be a voice crying in the desert: Make straight the way of the Lord. He prepared the people for the coming of the Lord, preparing his way in the desert. This is our vocation, too. We too should live in the desert, far from the world in its worldliness, preparing ourselves and the world for the coming of the Lord. There must be preparation for his coming in order to receive him well and enjoy his blessings. This preparation includes ourselves, together with all whom we can reach with our word and the example of our life, so that we may all be able to live a new life in the "Savior, who is Christ the Lord" (Lk 2:11).

Christ gives us a new kind of life, a life reconciled with God, a life at peace with God, which is something we cannot give to ourselves, for we are lost in sin and are far from God. Only the Son of God, our "Savior, who is Christ the Lord" (Lk 2:11), can free us from our sins, from our distance from God, and from his wrath for our sins.

Even once we have received Jesus Christ, we still need to go into the desert with John the Baptist to prepare the way of the Lord. Our life needs still more purification from worldliness, and the world also needs this same purification. Like John, we can help the world by our preaching and example.

Christ came so that we might have peace, so that we might be freed from sin and from the depression caused by guilt. If we take refuge in Christ in faith, especially through the sacrament of penance (Mt 18:18; Jn 20:23), he will cleanse us ever anew and restore us to his "peace which surpasses all understanding" (Phil 4:7).

There is nothing better in this world than living in peace with God, which Jesus Christ brings us through his death on the cross, where he suffered our penalty and thus freed us from the suffering caused by our sins. This gift of peace, which only comes through Jesus Christ, changes our life and will also change the world, transforming it into the Kingdom of God (Rev 11:15).

We, moreover, are to be the agents of this transformation by being transformed ourselves and by going into the desert with John to prepare the way of the Lord. Our preaching of Christ and the example of our life will transform the world, so that it may live in the peace of Christ, of which the angels sang at his birth, saying, "Glory to God in the highest, and on earth peace, good will toward men" (Lk 2:14 KJV).

EVANGELICAL POVERTY

"And they went with haste, and found Mary and Joseph, and the babe lying in a manger" (Lk 2:16).

St. Luke tells us that "Mary kept all these things, pondering them in her heart" (Lk 2:19). It is from her recollections that the evangelists learned the personal details of the birth of Christ.

We see the Savior of the world laid in a manger, born in a cave for animals, outside, on a trip, in the city of David, and announced to poor shepherds by an angel as "a Savior, who is Christ the Lord" (Lk 2:11). And at his birth, the angels sang, "Glory to God in the highest, and on earth peace, good will toward men" (Lk 2:14 KJV).

Christ the Lord, born this day in the city of David, is the Son of God, sent into the world by the Father to satisfy divine justice and shield us from the wrath of God for our sins. He did this by dying on the cross, suffering the death penalty due to our sins in place of us, so that God might thus be reconciled to us. Such great love has God for man that he sent his only Son to free us from our sins through his death on the cross, for only thus could God truly forgive our sins, being himself a just God. Former sins were forgiven ahead of time but not truly expiated until Christ came. A just retribution had to be paid, and sin punished, in order to be adequately expiated and properly forgiven. Jesus, the Savior of the world, did this for us. He paid the penalty for us, suffering himself the punishment due for our sins, so that we might go free from sin, free from punishment, free from guilt, to enjoy the freedom of the sons of God (Rom 8:21).

Christ came into the world, was born in a cave in Bethlehem, and was laid in a manger for this purpose. Our freedom from sin and guilt is in this child in the manger. The light of God that shines in our heart comes from this child.

Christ's suffering on the cross for our salvation began at his birth—that is, in the way in which he was born. He came in poverty, in the evangelical poverty that he himself would preach; and he did so as an expression of his total dedication to his Father in every aspect of his life. He did not come for the pleasures of this world but rather to serve his Father (Mt 6:24), renouncing all else, even a bed to sleep in and a house to be born in; and in this he is a model for us all.

THE POOR IN SPIRIT
REJOICE IN THE LORD

"…my spirit rejoices in God my Savior, for he has regarded the low estate of his handmaiden … he has put down the mighty from their thrones, and exalted those of low degree; he has filled the hungry with good things, and the rich he has sent away empty" (Lk 1:47–48,52–53).

Mary rejoices in the Lord. St. Paul says, "Rejoice in the Lord always. Again I say, Rejoice!" (Phil 4:4), and, "Finally, my brethren, rejoice in the Lord" (Phil 3:1), and, "Rejoice always" (1 Thess 5:16). A Christian rejoices in the Lord because he is saved, forgiven, has his guilt removed by Christ, is clothed by him in a splendid robe of righteousness (Is 61:10), and is justified by his faith in Christ, not by his own merits.

Salvation began in the body and spirit of the Virgin Mary. She conceived the Savior of the world through the power of the Holy Spirit; and therefore, she says, "My spirit rejoices in God my Savior" (Lk 1:47). True human happiness is in the Lord. The joy of our heart is in Jesus Christ, in his saving work within us. Even Hannah, the mother of Samuel, knew this happiness in the Lord, and said, "my heart exults in the Lord … I rejoice in thy salvation" (1 Sam 2:1).

We too rejoice in the Lord, for "The Lord is near" (Phil 4:5). We live in the nearness of the Lord. We live in moderation and silence in order to be recollected, focused on the Lord, and centered in prayer, meditation, contemplation, and spiritual joy. We prepare our heart for the Lord's coming. We want him to come into our heart. We want to receive him well, with much love, in a heart well prepared by meditation and contemplation.

Mary says that the Lord has "exalted those of low degree; he has filled the hungry with good things, and the rich he has sent away empty" (Lk 1:52–53). Here we see that the poor (Lk 6:20) and the poor in spirit (Mt 5:3) are especially blessed by God, and that "theirs is the kingdom of heaven" (Mt 5:3). God loves the poor, the poor in spirit, the humble, the *anawim*, those who have lost everything but God, and therefore possess God and rejoice in him to a very high degree. He has filled them with good things (Lk 1:53)—that is, those who love him with all their heart and all their soul (Mk 12:30). The anawim, the poor in spirit, are the truly happy ones who rejoice in the Lord more than all the rest. May we be among their number.

PERSECUTED
FOR BEING DIFFERENT

"…and you will be hated by all for my name's sake. But he who endures to the end will be saved" (Mt 10:22).

This is Jesus' prediction, that such will be our future, that we will be hated by all for his name's sake (Mt 10:22). Perhaps we do not experience this all the time, or perhaps we are not experiencing it right now, but it is always something on our horizon if we are true Christians—that is, persons born again in Jesus Christ. And so it is, because the majority will always follow and imitate the values and customs of the culture in which they live. But these values and mores are not always in accord with our faith or with the way God is directing us to live and behave. In such a conflict between the surrounding culture and God's most perfect will for us, the culture usually wins out, and most people follow it. Those, on the contrary, who remain faithful to the will of God and oppose the surrounding culture and its false and worldly values and customs will always be very few. Perhaps you will be the only one in your environment who will remain faithful to the will of God in many important things. In such a case, it would be normal for you to be persecuted, hated, and opposed, even by everyone, with no one taking your part or supporting you. "…and you will be hated by all," Jesus says, "for my name's sake" (Mt 10:22).

In such a case, you have to persevere until the end and give good witness to everyone. At times, you will be persecuted for your very *perseverance* and will have to flee to another city. Do so! Jesus tells us that there will always be a city to which you can flee and take refuge. "When they persecute you in one town," he says, "flee to the next; for truly, I say to you, you will not have gone through all the towns of Israel, before the Son of man comes" (Mt 10:23).

You will be truly blessed if you are thus persecuted for your faith in Jesus Christ and for your obedience to his will (1 Peter 4:13–14). God will give you a refuge, and he himself will be your refuge; and for having suffered for him, he will greatly bless you and will give you new and even better opportunities to live for him alone and to give good witness that will help many.

Such will be our new life as true Christians. We will no longer be of this world (Jn 17:14,16), nor will we any longer imitate its worldly customs, believe its false values or follow its endless quest for pleasure. We shall rather embrace the cross, and live its mystery, losing and hating our life in this world for the love of Christ (Mk 8:35; Jn 12:25).

A true Christian has been called out of the world by Christ, and therefore the world hates and persecutes him, as it hated and persecuted Christ (Jn 15:18–19; 17:14). "I have given them thy word," said Jesus to his Father, "and the world has hated them because they are not of the world, even as I am not of the world" (Jn 17:14). By being faithful in this situation, without trying to imitate the worldliness of the world, we will be sanctified and blessed by God. A contemplative life will naturally lead to persecution at times, because it is always the way of the few, and it rejects the world and its false values. This is part of the asceticism of this way of life.

Part III
The Desert Aroma:
The Mystical Dimension of Desert Living

Good News to the Poor

"The Spirit of the Lord is upon me, because he has anointed me to preach good news to the poor. He has sent me to proclaim release to the captives and recovering of sight to the blind, to set at liberty those who are oppressed, to proclaim the acceptable year of the Lord" (Lk 4:18–19; Is 61:1–2).

This is the scripture that St. Luke tells us Jesus read in the synagogue in Nazareth; and upon finishing the reading, he said, "Today this scripture has been fulfilled in your hearing" (Lk 4:21).

Jesus Christ came from the Father, where he lived eternally with him in ineffable splendor, in an embrace of divine love, united with him in the Holy Spirit. He was sent into the world to bring us this splendor, to introduce us into this light. He became incarnate, clothing himself in our flesh, to illuminate it from within with his divinity. His divine person illuminated his own flesh, his own human nature, divinizing it, and at the same time illuminated and divinized all human flesh in principle, if only we have contact with him by believing in him and imitating his life.

Jesus Christ came that we might walk with him in the light. He said, "I have come as light into the world, that whoever believes in me may not remain in darkness" (Jn 12:46). He does not want us to remain in darkness, but rather to walk with him in light (Jn 8:12). For this, he was anointed by the Spirit as our Messiah. He came to proclaim "recovery of sight to the blind" (Lk 4:18), that they might see his light. He came to announce freedom to those in captivity, that they might be freed from oppression. Hence, he said, "I am the light of the world; he who follows me will not walk in darkness, but will have the light of life" (Jn 8:12). He wants us to walk in this light, for we are those who have seen a great light (Is 9:1). We are to be born again in him (Jn 3:3) and live with his light shining in our heart (2 Cor 4:6). This is the good news that he brings to the poor.

It is the poor in spirit who will see and live in this light. They are the ones, the poor of Yahweh, the *anawim*, who receive and accept this good news with open hearts. They are the ones who are illuminated and divinized by Jesus Christ. This is because they have lost everything else and remain with

God alone as their only source of happiness and joy. Jesus invites us all to be the poor of the Lord, to leave all else to obtain the buried treasure and the pearl of great price, which can only be obtained by renouncing all else (Mt 13:44–46). His invitation to the rich young man is for all of us, so that we might live only for him (Mt 19:21).

Only in this way can we live in his light, purifying our heart of other lights, that it be illuminated only by him. By leaving everything for the love of God, we can enjoy this inner light, which the Messiah came into the world to give us. He wants us to love him with all our heart (Mk 12:30).

JOHN THE BAPTIST'S DESERT LIVING

"And the child grew and became strong in spirit, and he was in the deserts till the day of his manifestation to Israel" (Lk 1:80).

John the Baptist lived in desert places since his youth (Lk 1:80) and was there when the word of God came to him, calling him to be a prophet, to prepare the way of the Lord. St. Luke says that "the word of God came to John the son of Zechariah *in* the desert" (Lk 3:2).

What was he doing in the desert? Why did he choose to live where there was no life? Why did he want to live in earthly barrenness, in a cave, dressed not in civilized clothing, but rather in "a garment of camel's hair" with "a leather girdle around his waist" (Mt 3:4)? And why, instead of eating the normal food of civilized people, did he eat "locusts and wild honey" (Mt 3:4)? What was his motive for behaving in such an extraordinary manner, living in solitude, in desert places, with the vast and unencumbered desert horizon?

We know that he was a man of God with a mission from before his birth to "make ready for the Lord a people prepared" (Lk 1:17). He chose to live alone, in the desert, because there he could purify himself of his appetites and unite himself with God in prayer, and thus have a "mouth like a sharp sword" and be "a polished arrow" in the Lord's quiver (Is 49:2). He had to live with God *first* in order to be able to speak his word with power and effect. The Lord put his word into his mouth, and set him "over nations and over kingdoms, to pluck up and to break down, to destroy and to overthrow, to build and to plant" (Jer 1:10). Many will fight against him, but they shall not prevail against him for the Lord will be with him (Jer 1:19). He was a light to the nations to bring the truth and salvation of God unto the ends of the earth (Is 49:6). He came as a voice which cries in the desert to prepare the way of the Lord, to make straight his paths, to fill up every valley, and to make every mountain low (Is 40:3–4).

The desert is the best place for this kind of life. Earthly barrenness is the place *par excellence* for heavenly manifestations; and he not only ate wild honey but also knew the sweetness of God in his heart in these barren wastes with nothing else to take up his time, attention, or interest. There, he could live a solitary life with God alone, a life of prayer and contemplation, resting in the fullness of God and refreshed by it. It was a life of reading, study, and prayer. In the desert, God is closer.

We also are called to be the mouth of the Lord, like his sharp sword, to speak his truth, to awaken those who are asleep, and to convert hearts. For such a vocation, there is no better place than the desert, than solitude, than an earthly wasteland, where we experience heavenly manifestations and savor the sweetness of the presence of God in our heart. So did John live in the light, in the desert. He became a witness to the light (Jn 1:8). He is a model for all who seek God today, and he shows us how to find him, how to be his prophet. God is calling us in this way. He wants to reveal himself to us in the wasteland and then send us out to proclaim his truth. How do you respond to this invitation?

COME AWAY
TO A DESERT PLACE

"Come away by yourselves to a desert place, and rest a while. For many were coming and going, and they had no leisure even to eat. And they went away in the boat to a desert place by themselves" (Mk 6:31–32).

We see in the Gospels that Jesus frequently withdrew alone to the desert or to a mountain to pray (Mk 6:46; Lk 6:12). Before calling the twelve apostles, "he went out into the mountain to pray; and all night he continued in prayer to God. And when it was day, he called his disciples, and chose from them twelve" (Lk 6:12–13). Before doing something as important as calling his twelve apostles, he withdrew alone to pray, and we see that "all night he continued in prayer to God" (Lk 6:12). This is important. We see here the need that Jesus had for prayer, for spending time in contemplation with his Father, especially at night, or "in the morning, a great while before day" (Mk 1:35), in "a desert place" (Mk 1:35) or on a mountain (Lk 6:12).

And we see that he taught his apostles to do the same, saying to them, "Come away by yourselves to a desert place, and rest a while … And they went away in the boat to a desert place by themselves" (Mk 6:31–32). We thus learn that we also have the same need to withdraw alone to a desert place or to a mountain to pass the night, or part of the night, in silent, contemplative prayer.

Rising, therefore, "in the morning, a great while before day" (Mk 1:35) and going to a desert place to pray, our relationship with God is restored and grows. We enter into communion with him in love and light. At this time, we rest in Jesus Christ, who justifies us and clothes us with his own righteousness as with a splendid robe (Is 61:10). It is in Christ that we have the forgiveness of our sins and imperfections, the removal of our guilt and depression, and the restoration of God's peace in our heart. In him, we find a peace that the world cannot give (Jn 14:27) and that only comes to us when we believe in him, invoke the merits of his death for us on the cross, and then rise with him to new life in his resurrection. In contemplative prayer, especially "in the morning, a great while before day" (Mk 1:35), we reap the benefits of this renewal of ourselves in Christ.

In contemplative prayer, Christ fills us with light. He shines in our heart (2 Cor 4:6), and we contemplate his glory and are transformed "from glory to glory" in his image through this contemplation (2 Cor 3:18). It is in contemplation that we know his peace, which is a peace that the world cannot give (Jn 14:27). And so our relationship with Christ grows; and from this deepened relationship, we draw the inner strength we need to preach Christ with power and conviction for the salvation of the world

COMMUNION WITH
GOD
IN A DESERT PLACE

"And he said to them, Come ye yourselves apart into a desert place and rest a while ... And they departed into a desert place by ship privately ... And Jesus, when he came out, saw much people, and was moved with compassion toward them, because they were as sheep not having a shepherd: and he began to teach them many things" (Mk 6:31–32,34 KJV).

We see two things in this Gospel passage: 1) Jesus and his disciples seek a time of rest in a desert place, and 2) Jesus, as a good shepherd, desires to pasture his people, who are like sheep gone astray, without a shepherd.

Both Jesus and his disciples were very active in their ministry, but now he wants to withdraw from the multitude and rest for a while in a desert place, in silence and peace. Actually, Jesus did this quite often. He withdrew from his disciples and went off alone to a desert place to pray; and at least once he spent the entire night in prayer on a mountain: "And it came to pass in those days," says St. Luke, "that he went out into a mountain to pray, and continued all night in prayer to God" (Lk 6:12 KJV).

But today he takes his disciples with him as he goes off to a desert place to pray. This he also did on the mount of Transfiguration, when "he took with him Peter and John and James, and went up on the mountain to pray" (Lk 9:28), and he did it again in the garden of Gethsemane when he took these same three disciples, wishing them to be with him as he prayed (Mk 14:33).

Prayer in a desert place was essential for Jesus in two senses. First, as the eternal Word, the eternal Son of the Father, he lived in constant communion with his Father and the Holy Spirit, in which he as Son always related to his Father as a son relates to his father, even though he was of the same divine substance as the Father, and equal to him in divinity, being fully God. This intimate communion from all eternity with his Father is like contemplative prayer, a communion of life and love, without words or ideas. Second, as a

121

true man, Jesus also needed to pray, just as he needed to eat and sleep. This is because he had a human soul, containing a human mind and a human will as part of his human nature; and as prayer is necessary for a human soul, it was also necessary for him as a true man, even though he was a divine person, and therefore God. (Since he also had a divine nature, he also had a divine mind and a divine will, which pertained to his divine nature). In his prayer as a perfect man, Jesus Christ is our model for what our prayer should be.

Prayer, especially contemplative prayer, is fundamental for a human being if he wants to be complete and act as God wants him to act. The scriptures are filled with prayer; we need only refer to the psalms. We were made for contemplative prayer, to go apart to a desert place and commune with God. Thus do we find the peace that we long for and need, and the rest for our spirit, which renews us. Thus do we also find the love that we need and for which we were created. In a desert place, we can enter into communion with God, which gives rest to our spirit. It is like a sweet and restful dream. In contemplative prayer in a desert place, we rest in the arms of God, embraced and loved by God. And from this prayer in a desert place, we rise up well rested and refreshed in both body and spirit, with a peace not of this world. This is what Jesus did from all eternity as the eternal Word of the Father; and it is what he did as a true man in the desert places of Palestine. And today we also see that he takes his apostles with him to teach them too this necessity of their nature. Even in the midst of their ministry, when his "apostles gathered themselves together unto Jesus, and told him all things, both what they had done, and what they had taught ... he said unto them, Come ye yourselves apart into a desert place" (Mk 6:30–31 KJV).

We have the same need that Jesus had for contemplative prayer in a desert place. The attraction of the desert is the attraction of God. God draws us to the desert to be alone with him, to seek him, to enjoy his presence and love, and to be renewed and rejuvenated by our contact with him in silence and solitude, without distraction or noise, far from other people and obligations. In the desert, the heart can rest and experience the peace of God.

Monks make a whole life program out of these episodes when Jesus rested in desert places. This is their specialization. They are specialists, and their specialty is contemplative prayer in a desert place, far from the world. They create oases in the deserts of this world, places of contemplation, centers of spiritual refreshment, for those who labor and are heavy-laden (Mt 11:28).

The Contemplative Silence of St. Joseph the Worker

"Is not this the carpenter's son?" (Mt 13:55).

St. Joseph, the adopted father of Jesus Christ, was a poor carpenter, a worker, living a simple, humble, and austere life, a model for all of us.

Work has great value and dignity. The monastic tradition has always emphasized work of all kinds, but especially manual work, such as carpentry. Monasticism sees great value in simple manual work done in silence as a way of focusing the mind and body on a task at hand, while at the same time allowing the heart freedom to focus on God. We can contemplate while seated in silence for several hours during the day, but we can extend our prayer for many more hours through silent work. In this way, we can pray most of the day without fatigue while at the same time supporting ourselves or doing good for others.

St. Joseph is a symbol of this for us—that is, of the dignity of work, especially manual work. But St. Joseph, from whom we hear not even a single word in the Gospels, is also a symbol and model of contemplative silence.

The monastic ideal is a simple and austere life of contemplative silence, in which our contemplation is extended throughout the day in silent, contemplative work. We focus on God while we work with our hands. Monks have always imitated St. Joseph, the simple and silent workman, in their typical work of copying manuscripts and cultivating the land. They do this while living only for God in evangelical poverty and renouncing the pleasures of the world. So lived St. Joseph in poverty, silence, and work, loving God with all his heart.

Intellectual work, such as writing sermons or religious books, is also important, for it too quietly focuses our mind and heart on God. The silent preparation required for such work, as well as the work itself, is a form of meditation.

St. Joseph is also a model of silent, wordless, idealess contemplation, focused only on God, when we are seated in silence and are not working. Undoubtedly, he prayed in this way before the manger, in the cave of Bethlehem, far from the world, in the silence of the night, on the edge of the desert, in great simplicity and love, illuminated by the Word of God made flesh before him. This form of prayer, without words or ideas, is very important. In it we experience the love of God in a radiant way in our heart, filling us with peace and light. St. Joseph, the silent, is our model for this kind of passive, illuminated contemplation, the prayer of the heart, the prayer of union, in the silence of the night.

THE SIMPLICITY AND
POVERTY OF ST. JOSEPH

"And the shepherds went with haste, and found Mary and Joseph, and the babe lying in a manger" (Lk 2:16).

This, I believe, is the most beautiful scene in history. Jesus Christ, the only divine Son of God, was born in a stable and laid in a manger while angels sang over the plains of Bethlehem. And an angel of the Lord appeared to certain shepherds that night in that same region and surrounded them with splendor, announcing to them, "behold, I bring you good tidings of great joy, which shall be to all people. For unto you is born this day in the city of David a Saviour, who is Christ the Lord" (Lk 2:10–11).

St. Joseph was part of these holy events. He protected the Virgin Mary and this child who saves us from our sins. St. Joseph was notified by an angel that this child was conceived by the Holy Spirit and would "save his people from their sins" (Mt 1:21). Some thirty years later, he would die on a cross to complete his mission for our salvation. His death is the sacrifice that made satisfaction for our sins, which trouble us and separate us from God. He wants us to be free from them and made adopted sons of God in him, sharing his own splendor and happiness.

St. Joseph and the Virgin Mary were the two people closest to this child, and they lived in intimacy with him in faith and love; that is, they lived in intimacy with God through this child whom they raised.

Those days in Bethlehem were special. Everything was new and simple. The Holy Family was camping out in a cave, on the edge of the Judean desert, near Bethlehem, cooking over an open fire and warming themselves by the same fire, smelling the smoke from the fresh burning wood, living in great simplicity and evangelical poverty.

It was a holy poverty, which helped them to draw near to God, because God alone was the focus of their life in Bethlehem—even more so than later in Nazareth, because here at this time, Joseph had no work, nor was he known. His life was, therefore, quiet, silent, and simple. He lived in a silence full of God, without visits or conversations, except with Mary, and with the shepherds and Magi, who came in a spirit of awe and prayer to pay homage to the new-born king, lying in the manger. They were all there together around the manger, basking in the splendor of Christ the Lord. They all had the faith necessary to appreciate this child and to adore him in silence, receiving from him the light that their spirits craved, the forgiveness of their sins, and heavenly peace.

We too need this heavenly peace and the forgiveness of our sins or imperfections, which trouble our consciences. God knows our need and so sent us this child, Christ the Lord. Through our faith, love, and spirit of prayer and contemplation, we can be as close to these saving events as St. Joseph was.

This scene of the Bethlehem cave is not just something from past history. It is present for us through our faith and love, for the spiritual reality of this scene exists in every age, and every believer can see and experience its splendor in his heart. Christ is always present in all his mysteries when one has faith and love, when one draws near to him in his mysteries in a spirit of contemplation. We too can, like St. Joseph, contemplate the glory of this child, and be, like him, "transformed from glory to glory" in the very image of this splendid child, by the work of the Holy Spirit (2 Cor 3:18). We can thus bask in his splendor, and be illuminated from within by him, as was St. Joseph, day after day, night after night, camped out in this cave, spiritually illuminated by the Son of God.

If we live in holy and evangelical poverty, as did the Holy Family, completely focused on God and on his only Son, who lived in their midst, we will see a great light dawn within our hearts. It is the light of Christ (Jn 8:12), which transforms us and fills us with divinity. But to experience this light, we have to renounce other competing lights of this world, which drown out this one, unique light (Lk 8:14). So lived St. Joseph, giving us an example of the renunciation and evangelical poverty necessary to experience the splendor of Christ the Lord in our hearts.

Obedience to the will of God is also essential and necessary for experiencing God as a light in the heart. If we fail in something, we must confess it and dedicate ourselves anew to the service of God in the way he wishes. So lived St. Joseph, a model of simplicity and obedience for all, a man who lived in the nearness of God.

ST. BERNARD'S ASCETICAL-
MYSTICAL PATH

Wisdom "will feed him with the bread of understanding, and give him the water of wisdom to drink ... She will exalt him above his neighbors, and will open his mouth in the midst of the assembly" (Sir 15:3,5–6).

St. Bernard is the second founder of the Cistercian order. He chose for himself the authentic and traditional path of spirituality, namely, the ascetical-mystical path, and reached great heights of mysticism. He lived a contemplative-monastic life in his monastery of Clairvaux, and from time to time, leaving his monastery, he preached Christ all over Europe during the twelfth century, the golden age of Cistercian monasticism.

St. Bernard made Christ the only love of his life, the only spouse of his heart (2 Cor 11:2), his only Lord and Master (Mt 6:24), whom he served with all his heart, with a pure and undivided heart (1 Cor 7:32–34). He renounced the pleasures of this world so that Christ would be his only pleasure and so that his heart would be completely undivided in his love of him.

St. Bernard lived in silence and solitude with God in his monastery, living in the light of Christ, for he embraced the way of the cross and of asceticism, renouncing the pleasures of the world and of this life for those of the Kingdom of God and of the new creation. He knew that it is the way of asceticism that leads to mysticism, that it is by embracing the cross of Christ that we come to walk illuminated by the light of his resurrection.

St. Bernard was a contemplative but was also a man of the word. Filled with divine wisdom and light by walking in this authentic ascetical-mystical path, he kindled the hearts of the multitudes of Europe with the love of God. His whole life was Christ and the contemplation of his glory (2 Cor 3:18) and sweetness. It was a life of faith, not of justification by works. It was an ascetical life, not a life of the delights of this world. It was a life of prayer, fasting, and love, and so did he arrive at the heights of mystical experience and lived in the love of God.

St. Bernard is a model for all who want to live a contemplative, monastic life, a life that contemplates the glory of Christ, which he gave us to contemplate. "The glory which thou hast given me I have given to them," Jesus said (Jn 17:22). We should, as St. Bernard, contemplate this glory by taking the same path he took, the ascetical-mystical path, the path of renouncing the entertainments and diversions of this world, to live in the new creation. In this way, we will be filled with the glory that Christ has given us and will be able to contemplate its light.

Jesus said, "Father, I desire that they also, whom thou hast given me, may be with me where I am, to behold my glory which thou hast given me" (Jn 17:24). Christ wants us to be with him where he is. Why? To contemplate his glory, as did St. Bernard. Christ wants us to remain in this glory, in this love. "As the Father has loved me, so have I loved you; remain in my love," Jesus said (Jn 15:9). Thus lived St. Bernard, in the light of Christ, basking in his light and departing periodically from his cloister to preach this love of Christ to the world, to kindle the world with the flame of divine love that burned his own heart.

Such was the rhythm of the life of St. Bernard, a model for us. He lived in silence and solitude, basking in the splendor of divine love through his life in Jesus Christ. He was renewed through living the mystery of the cross and renunciation. And he walked in the splendor of the risen Christ, rising with him to new life. Then, from time to time, he came out of his cloister to preach Christ and the love of God to the world.

By living in this way, St. Bernard became like the personified wisdom of the book of Sirach: he exhaled perfume, the perfume of his contemplation. "Like cinnamon and rosewood I exhaled perfume, and like exquisite myrrh I poured out aroma" (Sir 24:15). So did the wisdom of St. Bernard's ascetical-mystical life feed "him with the bread of understanding [and] give him the water of wisdom to drink" (Sir 15:3). By living in this way, he was exalted above his companions; and in the midst of the assembly, he was given the word. And so did he find joy, and the crown of glory (Sir 15:5–6).

We can imitate this life. St. Bernard was like a "column of smoke," rising out of the desert, "perfumed with myrrh and frankincense," and "with all the fragrant powders of the merchant" (Ct 3:6). He rose out of the desert, leaning on his beloved (Ct 8:5). He was perfumed by living the ascetical-mystical life, contemplating the glory that Christ had given him. We too can be transformed "from glory to glory" by this contemplation (2 Cor 3:18).

It is as though we were sleeping with Christ, like "a bag of myrrh, that lies between my breasts" (Ct 1:13), on a bed of flowers (Ct 1:16), in a house, whose beams are of cedar, and whose rafters are cypress (Ct 1:17); it is like a house, moreover, which is built upon a "mountain of myrrh" and a "hill of frankincense" (Ct 4:6). In this house, we pass the night with our divine spouse, "Until the day breathes and the shadows flee" (Ct 4:6). Even the scent of our garments is "like the scent of Lebanon" (Ct 4:11) because we are perfumed by our contemplation of the glory of Christ. Even our breath is perfumed. We exhale perfume (Sir 25:15), and our divine spouse says, "the scent of your breath [is] like apples" (Ct 7:8); and so we say, "Sustain me with raisins, refresh me with apples; for I am sick with love" (Ct 2:5).

Such is the authentic and traditional path of spirituality, which we are invited to take.

ST. BERNARD OF CLAIRVAUX
AND THE CONTEMPLATION
OF GOD'S GLORY

"The glory which thou hast given me I have given to them, that they may be one even as we are one" (Jn 7:22).

The Cistercian Order, a monastic order, was founded in 1098 by Robert of Molesme, Alberic, and Stephen Harding in Citeaux, France. Their life was so strict and austere that their greatest worry and fear was that they would never get any new recruits, for although their neighbors admired them for their piety, they were horrified at their way of life (*Exordium of Citeaux*, 2; *The Little Exordium*, 16). Their problem, however, was solved when one day there appeared at the gates of the monastery, Bernard, with his four brothers and twenty-seven other friends, all seeking to enter as novices. Bernard came to be the abbot of a new foundation in Clairvaux, France, and became a great preacher and writer of the love of God. The Gospel text quoted above well describes his spirit of love for God.

Christ gave us his glory, which is the same glory which the Father gave to him. He lives in this glory. He wants us also to live in this same glory. It is the glory of the love of God in our heart, which we have through Jesus Christ. The *same* love with which the Father loves the Son from all eternity is now also in *us* through Jesus Christ. The Father loves us as he loves his only Son. This is why the Father sent Jesus Christ into the world—so that the love which the Father has for the *Son* might also be in *us*. Jesus prayed to his Father, saying, "I made known to them thy name, and I will make it known, that the love with which thou hast loved *me* may be in *them*, and I in them" (Jn 17:26). It is the Trinitarian love, the love which exists within the Blessed Trinity, which we now have through Jesus Christ. It is a participation in the divine love which eternally flows between the Father and the Son.

It is Jesus Christ who communicates this love to us, especially in the eucharist. He comes to live in our heart through his body and blood which we eat and drink. Then, in contemplative prayer, he deepens this love in our soul. He himself comes to live in us, bringing us the love of the Father (Jn 14:23). He who is one with his Father comes to be one with us. He unites himself to us in the eucharist, and so we are united at the same time with the Father (Jn 14:20).

In contemplative prayer we see his glory, the glory which the Father has given Christ, and this glory also shines in us, illuminating us from within. St. Bernard lived for this glory. This is why he became a monk, leaving behind everything else in the world to live for and in this glory. Hence he lived a life of silence within an enclosure, dedicating himself to singing the praises of God in the monastic choir, and living the cloistered life, when he was not on one of his many preaching missions throughout Europe. The austerity of this life energized him, for it purified him for God, for the contemplation of his glory. Living for God alone, he lived in his love and wrote of the divine love which filled his heart.

St. Bernard is an example for us all. Everyone can live in the love of God and dedicate himself to contemplating his glory. Christ gave us this glory so that we might contemplate it and thus grow in his image (2 Cor 3:18). "The glory which thou hast given me," said Jesus, "I have given to them" (Jn 17:22). And, "Father, I desire that they also, whom thou hast given me, may be with me where I am, to behold my glory which thou hast given me in thy love for me" (Jn 17:24). To *behold* his glory is to *contemplate* it. The contemplative life, which is the monastic life, is dedicated to contemplating God's glory. And we have seen this glory through Jesus Christ. "And the word became flesh," says St. John, "and dwelt among us, full of grace and truth; we have beheld his glory, glory as of the only Son from the Father" (Jn 1:14). We live for this vision of his glory. We renounce everything else, as did St. Bernard, to see and contemplate this glory, to live in this glory. And it is by means of Jesus Christ that we receive this glory, this fullness of God—especially when we receive him in Holy Communion. "And from his fullness we have all received, grace upon grace," as St. John affirms (Jn 1:16). And this fullness, this glory, transforms us as we contemplate it. "But we all, with open face beholding as in a glass the glory of the Lord, are changed into the same image from glory to glory, even by the Spirit of the Lord" (2 Cor 3:18 KJV).

THE NUPTIAL LOVE
OF THE VIRGIN MARY

"And a great portent appeared in heaven, a woman clothed with the sun, with the moon under her feet, and on her head a crown of twelve stars (Rev 12:1).

After her death, the Blessed Virgin Mary was assumed body and soul into heaven as a special privilege because she was the Mother of God. This text of the Apocalypse has traditionally been understood as a description of her in her glory after her Assumption. She is a beautiful and glorious woman, "clothed with the sun, with the moon under her feet, and on her head a crown of twelve stars" (Rev 12:1). She is beautiful, the bride of God himself. She is "terrible as an army with banners" (Ct 6:4). She is the fulfillment of the bride of the Song of Songs, and her bridegroom is God. In this, she is a type and example for us all—human beings who can have a nuptial relationship with God. Jesus Christ has united us to God, and now we are like his bride. We see in the Virgin Mary our own ideal relationship with God, and all this is described symbolically in the Song of Songs. The bridegroom is God; we are the bride, and so also—and in the most perfect sense—is the Virgin Mary. As we marvel at her beauty and at the beauty of her relationship with God, we are inspired to develop a similar relationship.

Hence, filled with admiration, we say, "Who is this that looks forth like the dawn, fair as the moon, bright as the sun, terrible as an army with banners?" (Ct 6:10). Her great beauty, which shines in heaven, comes from her loving relationship with God. His love beautifies her. Even during her earthly life, she lived alone with this great love of her heart. She lived in a desert of solitude with God, reclining upon him. "Who is this," we say, "that is coming up from the desert, leaning upon her beloved?" (Ct 8:5). It is the Virgin Mary, all perfumed with the love of God. Truly, "What is that coming up from the desert, like a column of smoke, perfumed with myrrh and frankincense, with all the fragrant powders of the merchant?" (Ct 3:6). It is the Virgin Mary coming up from her contemplation, all perfumed with the fragrance of God.

Thus does the love of God beautify us. It gives us the odor of sanctity, and the desert is the place *par excellence* for this loving encounter with God. This is why the desert, with its solitude and silence, has always been the favorite place of monks in their desire to live in the love of God. And the Virgin Mary, in her solitude with God, wrapped up in his love, is their model. We too can be all perfumed with the fragrance of God, the odor of sanctity, alone with him in contemplation in the desert. This is because our bridegroom is "like a gazelle or a young stag upon the mountains of spices" (Ct 8:14). He communicates his fragrance to us, and we exhale perfume. "Like cinnamon and camel's thorn," we say with her, "I exhaled the aroma of spices, and like choice myrrh I spread a pleasant odor" (Sir 24:15). She is all perfumed with the aroma of her contemplation in solitude. She is "like the fragrance of frankincense in the tabernacle" (Sir 24:15), and her "blossoms became glorious and abundant fruit" (Sir 24:17). So she says to us, "Come to me, you who desire me, and eat your fill of my fruits. For the remembrance of me is sweeter than honey, and my inheritance sweeter than the honeycomb" (Sir 24:19–20). She is the great model of a person who is full of God, made resplendent by his love. Hence in this great love, she "grew tall like a cedar in Lebanon, and like a cypress on the heights of Hermon." She "grew tall like a palm tree in Engedi, and like the rose plants in Jericho" (Sir 24:13–14).

She has her secret hideaway in a forest of aromatic trees (Ct 4:6), with beams of cedar and rafters of cypress (Ct 1:16), and she sleeps on a bed of flowers (Ct 1:16), with her beloved like a bag of myrrh between her breasts (Ct 1:13). Her beloved goes to this hideaway to be alone with her in love, and he says, "Until the day breathes and the shadows flee, I will hie me to the mountain of myrrh and the hill of frankincense" (Ct 4:6).

He is for her "As an apple tree among the trees of the wood" (Ct 2:3), and she eats raisins and is refreshed with apples, for she is sick with love (Ct 2:5), and the scent of her breath is like apples (Ct 7:8). She lives in remote places, to be alone with the beloved of her heart. And he calls to her to "Depart from the peak of Amana, from the peak of Senir and Hermon, from the dens of lions, from the mountains of leopards" (Ct 4:8). Because she lives in these remote forest hideaways, the scent of her garments is like the scent of Lebanon (Ct 4:11). She also has a cabin, where "The mandrakes give forth fragrance," and she says, "over our doors are all choice fruits" (Ct 7:13).

So lives the Blessed Virgin Mary with the beloved of her heart; and so should we also live.

THE NEW JERUSALEM

"And in the spirit he carried me away to a great, high mountain, and showed me the holy city Jerusalem coming down out of heaven from God, having the glory of God, its radiance like a most rare jewel, like jasper, clear as crystal" (Rev 21:10–11).

This is the vision of the New Jerusalem, the city of gold and light, the city of splendor, diaphanous as crystal. It is the city of our spirit. It is our future, for it is the heavenly city to which we are headed, the city of those who are saved in Jesus Christ. But we can live in this city even now in spirit if we are saved in Christ and are contemplatives. It is a city of light and peace, the light and peace which we have in God through faith. By faith we are justified and made resplendent with the splendor of Christ himself, and the dwelling place of our spirit is with him in this city, diaphanous as crystal. We are illuminated by him like a rock crystal, pierced by a ray of sunlight at midday.

This city is overwhelmingly beautiful. "The wall was built of jasper, while the city was pure gold, clear as glass" (Rev 21:18). "And the twelve gates were twelve pearls ... and the street of the city was pure gold, transparent as glass" (Rev 21:21). This is our ideal, to live in this city of splendor and light, "diaphanous as crystal" (Rev 21:11). The saints live there now much of their time, even in this life, for Christ illuminates them from within (2 Cor 4:6), and they walk in his light (Jn 8:12). It is Christ who is for us the light that shines in the darkness of this world (Jn 1:5). In his incarnation we have seen his glory, "glory as the only Son from the Father" (Jn 1:14). And because he illuminates us, we receive from his fullness grace upon grace (Jn 1:16). We walk in his light (Jn 8:12).

This city, this dwelling place of our spirit both now and in the future, is illuminated by God himself and by the Lamb (Rev 21, 23). Its splendor does not come from the sun, but from the Lord. God and the Lamb are our lights that shine in our hearts in this city, illuminating us from within with a light not of this world and putting us in a splendor which is not from here below. It is our contemplation which illuminates us, for that is when God shines most powerfully within us.

This is why we love solitude—to bask in this splendor and not lose it by talking. Our mornings can be luminous if we bask in this light in solitude. It is Jesus Christ who clothes us with his own splendor when we believe in him and live for him alone.

This city has great attraction, and "By its light shall the nations walk" (Rev 21:24).

We can live more and more in this light, in this city of splendor, though faith and through contemplation in silence and solitude far from the world and its distractions and noise. This is why many have sought out a solitary life in the desert or in the mountains—to live only for and with Christ and to walk in his light.

If we are citizens of this city, we can attract others too, to enjoy its light with us through their faith and life of prayer. Those who live in this city become lights for the rest, beacons shining in the darkness, showing the way (Phil 2:15; Mt 5:14–16).

A solitary life can be a luminous life much of the time if we live in Jesus Christ in silence and prayer, in fasting and simplicity, in poverty and service to others.

And when our life in this world comes to an end, if we are saved by Christ, we go to this heavenly city, the New Jerusalem, to live there in a far more complete way than now. And finally, when Christ comes again in his glory, it will be in the New Jerusalem that we will all live together in splendor with our glorified bodies.

A Kingdom
of Light and Peace

"And behold, you will conceive in your womb and bear a son, and you shall call his name Jesus. He will be great, and will be called Son of the Most High; and the Lord God will give to him the throne of his father David, and he will reign over the house of Jacob for ever; and of his kingdom there will be no end" (Lk 1:31–33).

With this chapter we come to the end of *Desert Living*. We explored religious life, particularly the eremitic life, as an ascetical-mystical journey to union with God. We looked first at its general principles, then explored its ascetical dimension, and finally, its mystical dimension. Today, as I write this, we are celebrating the Queenship of Mary and so recall that we are living in the Kingdom of God, a kingdom which has both a King and a Queen. Religious life, the eremitic life, the ascetical-mystical path, has brought us to the heart of this kingdom of light and peace.

The Virgin Mary, whom we honor today as Queen, gave birth to a son to whom would be given the throne of his father David. "...he will reign over the house of Jacob for ever, and of his kingdom there will be no end" (Lk 1:32–33). This is the Messianic kingdom which he has inaugurated and in which we now live. When he was born, the people who walked in darkness saw a great light; and on those who dwelt in the land of the shadow of death, light shined (Is 9:2).

The Virgin Mary is Queen because she is the mother of this great King who has an eternal kingdom of light and peace upon the earth. His birth gave glory to God in the highest and brought peace on earth. Through him we can all be born anew as new men (Eph 2:22–24) in a new creation (2 Cor 5:17; Rev 21:5). And this Queen is our mother, for we have been made adopted sons of God in her son. If he is King over the whole earth, bringing it peace and joy, she is its Queen, shining in his light.

If we want peace, we should take refuge in him, for he brought peace on earth in his birth and is the Prince of Peace. "Of the increase of his government and of peace there will be no end, upon the throne of David, and over his kingdom" (Is 9:7). Who does not want peace in his heart, peace in his life? For this he came to the earth—to establish a kingdom of universal peace for all who believe in him, take refuge in him in their problems, and obey and serve him with all their heart. He is the Prince of Peace. "Peace I leave with you; my peace I give to you," he said; "not as the world gives do I give to you" (Jn 14:27). His peace is an interior peace, in the depths of the spirit. It is a divine presence in us which gives us joy. It is the presence of Christ shining in our heart, illuminating it (2 Cor 4:6). "…justified by faith, we have peace with God through our Lord Jesus Christ" (Rom 5:1). We can live in this peace of his kingdom over all the earth. "I have said this to you, that in me you may have peace. In the world you have tribulation; but be of good cheer, I have overcome the world" (Jn 16:33). This is why we take refuge in him in our tribulation in this world, and he restores our peace.

The Queen of this peace is Mary. If we live in peace with Christ, we also live with her in her peace and joy in the Lord.

How important it is for us to live in this kingdom of universal peace with the Prince of Peace! It is a kingdom of light which shines in us also. If we lose this peace, and if we take refuge in him, in his due time he will restore us again and will give us even more peace than before. In him, indeed, is our peace.

Appendix
Official Church Teaching on Celibacy and Marriage

What follows are quotations from official Church documents, downloaded from the Vatican website (www.vatican.va). The highlighted passages give the kernel of the Church's teaching on this subject, namely, that celibacy for the Kingdom of God is an objectively higher call than Christian marriage.

Familiaris consortio, 16, Apostolic exhortation of Pope John Paul II

Virginity or celibacy, by liberating the human heart in a unique way, "so as to make it burn with greater love for God and all humanity," bears witness that the Kingdom of God and His justice is that pearl of great price which is preferred to every other value no matter how great, and hence must be sought as the only definitive value. **It is for this reason that the Church, throughout her history, has always defended the superiority of this charism to that of marriage**, by reason of the wholly singular link which it has with the Kingdom of God.

In spite of having renounced physical fecundity, the celibate person becomes spiritually fruitful, the father and mother of many, cooperating in the realization of the family according to God's plan.

Vita Consecrata, 18; 32, Apostolic exhortation of Pope John Paul II

18. In the countenance of Jesus, the "image of the invisible God" (*Col* 1:15) and the reflection of the Father's glory (cf. *Heb* 1:3), we glimpse the depths of an eternal and infinite love which is at the very root of our being. Those who let themselves be seized by this love cannot help abandoning everything to

follow him (cf. *Mk* 1:16–20; 2:14; 10:21, 28). Like Saint Paul, they consider all else as loss "because of the surpassing worth of knowing Jesus Christ," by comparison with which they do not hesitate to count all things as "refuse," in order that they "may gain Christ" (*Phil* 3:8). They strive to become one with him, taking on his mind and his way of life. This leaving of everything and following the Lord (cf. *Lk* 18:28) is a worthy programme of life for all whom he calls, in every age. The evangelical counsels, by which Christ invites some people to share his experience as the chaste, poor and obedient One, call for and make manifest in those who accept them *an explicit desire to be totally conformed to him*. Living "in obedience, with nothing of one's own and in chastity," consecrated persons profess that Jesus is the model in whom every virtue comes to perfection. His way of living in chastity, poverty and obedience appears as the most radical way of living the Gospel on this earth, a way which may be called *divine*, for it was embraced by him, God and man, as the expression of his relationship as the Only-Begotten Son with the Father and with the Holy Spirit. **This is why Christian tradition has always spoken of the objective superiority of the consecrated life**. Nor can it be denied that the practice of the evangelical counsels is also a particularly profound and fruitful way of sharing in *Christ's mission*, in imitation of the example of Mary of Nazareth, the first disciple, who willingly put herself at the service of God's plan by the total gift of self. Every mission begins with the attitude expressed by Mary at the Annunciation: "Behold, I am the handmaid of the Lord; let it be done to me according to your word" (*Lk* 1:38).

32. Within this harmonious constellation of gifts, each of the fundamental states of life is entrusted with the task of expressing, in its own way, one or other aspect of the one mystery of Christ. While *the lay life* has *a particular mission* of ensuring that the Gospel message is proclaimed in the temporal sphere, in the sphere of ecclesial communion *an indispensable ministry is carried out by those in Holy Orders*, and in a special way by Bishops. The latter have the task of guiding the People of God by the teaching of the word, the administration of the sacraments and the exercise of sacred power in the service of ecclesial communion, which is an organic communion, hierarchically structured. **As a way of showing forth the Church's holiness, it is to be recognized that the consecrated life, which mirrors Christ's own way of life, has an objective superiority**. Precisely for this reason, it is an especially rich manifestation of Gospel values **and a more complete expression of the Church's purpose**, which is the sanctification of humanity. The consecrated life proclaims and in a certain way anticipates the future age, when the fullness of the Kingdom of heaven, already present in its first fruits and in mystery, will be achieved, and when the children of the resurrection will take neither wife nor husband, but will be like the angels of God (cf. *Mt* 22:30). **The Church has always taught**

the pre-eminence of perfect chastity for the sake of the Kingdom, and rightly considers it the "door" of the whole consecrated life. She also shows great esteem for the vocation to marriage, which makes spouses "witnesses to and cooperators in the fruitfulness of Holy Mother Church, who signify and share in the love with which Christ has loved his Bride and because of which he delivered himself up on her behalf."

Optatam totius, 10, Vat. II, decree on priestly training

10. Students who follow the venerable tradition of celibacy according to the holy and fixed laws of their own rite are to be educated to this state with great care. For renouncing thereby the companionship of marriage for the sake of the kingdom of heaven (cf. Matt. 19:12), **they embrace the Lord with an undivided love altogether befitting the new covenant,** bear witness to the resurrection of the world to come (cf. Luke 20:36), and obtain a most suitable aid for the continual exercise of that perfect charity whereby they can become all things to all men in their priestly ministry. Let them deeply realize how gratefully that state ought to be received, not, indeed, only as commanded by ecclesiastical law, but as a precious gift of God for which they should humbly pray. Through the inspiration and help of the grace of the Holy Spirit let them freely and generously hasten to respond to this gift.

Students ought rightly to acknowledge the duties and dignity of Christian matrimony, which is a sign of the love between Christ and the Church. **Let them recognize, however, the surpassing excellence of virginity consecrated to Christ,** so that with a maturely deliberate and generous choice they may consecrate themselves to the Lord by a complete gift of body and soul.

They are to be warned of the dangers that threaten their chastity especially in present-day society. Aided by suitable safeguards, both divine and human, let them learn to integrate their renunciation of marriage in such a way that they may suffer in their lives and work not only no harm from celibacy but rather acquire a deeper mastery of soul and body and a fuller maturity, and more perfectly receive the blessedness spoken of in the Gospel.

Presbyteriorum ordinis, 16, Vat. II, decree on the ministry and life of priests:

16. (Celibacy is to be embraced and esteemed as a gift). Perfect and perpetual continence for the sake of the Kingdom of Heaven, commended by Christ the Lord and through the course of time as well as in our own days freely accepted and observed in a praiseworthy manner by many of the faithful, is held by

the Church to be of great value in a special manner for the priestly life. It is at the same time a sign and a stimulus for pastoral charity and a special source of spiritual fecundity in the world. Indeed, it is not demanded by the very nature of the priesthood, as is apparent from the practice of the early Church and from the traditions of the Eastern Churches, where, besides those who with all the bishops, by a gift of grace, choose to observe celibacy, there are also married priests of highest merit. This holy synod, while it commends ecclesiastical celibacy, in no way intends to alter that different discipline which legitimately flourishes in the Eastern Churches. It permanently exhorts all those who have received the priesthood and marriage to persevere in their holy vocation so that they may fully and generously continue to expend themselves for the sake of the flock commended to them.

Indeed, celibacy has a many-faceted suitability for the priesthood. For the whole priestly mission is dedicated to the service of a new humanity which Christ, the victor over death, has aroused through his Spirit in the world and which has its origin "not of blood, nor of the will of the flesh, nor of the will of man but of God" (Jn 1:13). **Through virginity, then, or celibacy observed for the Kingdom of Heaven, priests are consecrated to Christ by a new and exceptional reason. They adhere to him more easily with an undivided heart, they dedicate themselves more freely in him and through him to the service of God and men, and they more expeditiously minister to his Kingdom and the work of heavenly regeneration, and thus they are apt to accept, in a broad sense, paternity in Christ**. In this way they profess themselves before men as willing to be dedicated to the office committed to them—namely, to commit themselves faithfully to one man and to show themselves as a chaste virgin for Christ and thus to evoke the mysterious marriage established by Christ, and fully to be manifested in the future, in which the Church has Christ as her only Spouse. They give, moreover, a living sign of the world to come, by a faith and charity already made present, in which the children of the resurrection neither marry nor take wives.

For these reasons, based on the mystery of Christ and his mission, celibacy, which first was recommended to priests, later in the Latin Church was imposed upon all who were to be promoted to sacred orders. This legislation, pertaining to those who are destined for the priesthood, this holy synod again approves and confirms, fully trusting this gift of the Spirit so fitting for the priesthood of the New Testament, freely given by the Father, provided that those who participate in the priesthood of Christ through the sacrament of Orders-and also the whole Church-humbly and fervently pray for it. This sacred synod also exhorts all priests who, in following the example of Christ, freely receive sacred celibacy as a grace of God, that they magnanimously and wholeheartedly adhere to it, and that persevering faithfully in it, they may acknowledge this outstanding gift of the Father which is so openly praised and extolled by the Lord. Let them keep before their eyes the great mysteries signified by it and fulfilled in it. Insofar as perfect continence is thought by many men to be impossible in our times, to that extent priests should all the more humbly and steadfastly pray with the Church for that grace of fidelity, which is never denied those who seek it, and use all the supernatural and natural aids available. They should especially seek, lest they omit them, the ascetical norms which have been proved by the experience of the Church and which are scarcely less necessary in the contemporary world. This holy synod asks not only priests but all the faithful that they might receive this precious gift of priestly celibacy in their hearts and ask of God that he will always bestow this gift upon his Church.

Lumen gentium, chap. 5, par. 42, Vatican II, decree on the Church

Likewise, the holiness of the Church is fostered in a special way by the observance of the counsels proposed in the Gospel by Our Lord to His disciples. An **eminent position** among these is held by **virginity** or the celibate state. This is a precious gift of divine grace given by the Father to certain souls, whereby they **may devote themselves to God alone the more easily**, due to an **undivided heart**. This perfect continency, out of desire for the kingdom of heaven, has always been held in **particular honor** in the Church. The reason for this was and is that perfect continency for the love of God is an incentive to charity, and is certainly a particular source of spiritual fecundity in the world.

Sacerdotalis coelibatus, 20–23, Pope Paul VI, encyclical on priestly celibacy

Matrimony and Celibacy

20. Matrimony, according to the will of God, continues the work of the first creation; and considered within the total plan of salvation, it even acquired a new meaning and a new value. Jesus, in fact, has restored its original dignity, has honored it and has raised it to the dignity of a sacrament and of a mysterious symbol of His own union with the Church. Thus, Christian couples walk together toward their heavenly fatherland in the exercise of mutual love, in the fulfillment of their particular obligations, and in striving for the sanctity proper to them. **But Christ, "Mediator of a superior covenant," has also opened a new way, in which the human creature adheres wholly and**

directly to the Lord, and is concerned only with Him and with His affairs; thus, he manifests in a clearer and more complete way the profoundly transforming reality of the New Testament.

Christ's Example

21. Christ, the only Son of the Father, by the power of the Incarnation itself was made Mediator between heaven and earth, between the Father and the human race. Wholly in accord with this mission, **Christ remained throughout His whole life in the state of celibacy, which signified His total dedication to the service of God and men**. This deep concern between celibacy and the priesthood of Christ is reflected in those whose fortune it is to share in the dignity and mission of the Mediator and eternal Priest; **this sharing will be more perfect the freer the sacred minister is from the bonds of flesh and blood.**

The Motive for Celibacy

22. Jesus, who selected the first ministers of salvation, wished them to be introduced to the understanding of the "mysteries of the kingdom of heaven," but He also wished them to be coworkers with God under a very special title, and His ambassadors. He called them friends and brethren, for whom He consecrated Himself so that they might be consecrated in truth; **He promised a more than abundant recompense to anyone who should leave home, family, wife and children for the sake of the kingdom of God.** More than this, in words filled with mystery and hope, **He also commended an even more perfect consecration to the kingdom of heaven by means of celibacy, as a special gift.** The motive of this response to the divine call is the kingdom of heaven; similarly, this very kingdom, the Gospel and the name of Christ motivate those called by Jesus to undertake the work of the apostolate, freely accepting its burdens, that they may participate the more closely in His lot.

23. To them this is the mystery of the newness of Christ, of all that He is and stands for; **it is the sum of the highest ideals of the Gospel and of the kingdom**; it is a particular manifestation of grace, which springs from the Paschal mystery of the Savior. This is what makes the choice of celibacy desirable and worthwhile to those called by our Lord Jesus. **Thus they intend not only to participate in His priestly office, but also to share with Him His very condition of living.**

Works Cited

Coriden, J. A.

Thomas J. Green, and Donald F. Heintschel. *The Code of Canon Law: A Text and Commentary*. Commissioned by the Canon Law Society of America. New York: Paulist, 1985.

Marchetti-Salvatori, B.

"Despojarse." Ermanno Ancilli. *Diccionario de Espiritualidad*. 3 vols. Barcelona: Herder, 1987.

Breinigsville, PA USA
04 November 2009
226971BV00001B/3/P

9 781440 176555